A NIPPER'S TALE

Alan Rampling

Published by

**MELROSE
BOOKS**

An Imprint of Melrose Press Limited
St Thomas Place, Ely
Cambridgeshire
CB7 4GG, UK
www.melrosebooks.co.uk

FIRST EDITION

Copyright © Alan Rampling 2016

The Author asserts his moral right to

be identified as the author of this work

Cover designed by Melrose Books

ISBN 978-1-911280-08-8
epub 978-1-911280-09-5
mobi 978-1-911280-10-1

Printed and bound in Great Britain by:
TJ International Ltd, Padstow, Cornwall

MIX
Paper from
responsible sources
FSC
www.fsc.org   FSC® C013056

ME

I like Bond minis and cars that are old
Like Bentleys and vintage Rolls Royces.
I love isolation, but not desolation
I like manners and soft spoken voices.

I like fishing, walking and painting,
I like warmth and my own comfy bed.
Don't like people with inflated egos
Designer names and so-called street cred.

I hate greedy people who always want more:
More money, more clothes, more stuff.
I'll stick to my own saying and won't veer off
That only just, is just enough.

Don't like crowds or shopping,
Nor people that flaunt their wealth.
I treasure my home, my family,
My past, my future, my health.

I hate waste, I hate haste, I like music,
I like summer and the sound of a bee,
Water in streams that ripple,
The new spring green on a tree.

I'm not too keen on religion.
I like to stand and stare
And have the time to write a rhyme.
I love people who really care.

I don't like people who copy,
Who are intolerant or moan.
It proves they are jealous
And have no mind of their own.

I don't like smokers, fast talkers or dogs
And scroungers who want things for free.
This variety of likes and dislikes
Is just a small slice of me.

CONTENTS

PREFACE

Why do I want to write this book about me? I'm nothing special, I've not invented anything, saved anyone, nor killed anyone. I don't think, but I believe everyone has a story to tell. Mine was influenced by a visit to a place that I still hold very dear to my heart – Mercer Street in Preston, Lancashire.

A visit back to this, my childhood home, stirred some deep memories of a bygone era. A time just after the Second World War when great adjustment took place. We were free to enjoy ourselves and slowly built up what the previous years had taken away. Being a young lad then, I was indeed given the freedom to be myself: play out until dark, beyond sometimes. To explore, develop my imagination, to be allowed to learn in my own time and way. Always arriving home with chapped legs, a few cuts and grazes and, on occasions, a black eye. I was always sure of understanding and love that my mum and grandma gave to me. Sometimes getting told off for going 'a bit too far', but always a kiss at bedtime. Alas, now the street has been demolished and replaced by some faceless looking flats, and where my house was is now a huge green electricity sub-station.

Sat in my car viewing my childhood world, where enemies became friends one day and friends became enemies the next, brought back great volumes of pleasure. I could hear my little friends calling for me after tea. We would run around until we were almost sick, getting up to mischief, but not harming anyone nor anything. Just being kids held together with strips of Elastoplast.

Thinking of these things and more brought a happiness that I have been lucky enough to have experienced and have the capability of an excellent memory for people and places to recall, and also a sort of sadness that it has all gone, and in many cases, not replaced by anything better. We didn't have computers, ipads, phones, discs, videos, smart this and that and very little cash. What I had was love, understanding and a great feeling of contentment that no amount of money could buy: to be inventive by constructive play. This book recalls a lot of childhood adventures that came pouring out of my deepest memory through to school work, college and later life.

If only I could do it all again.

CHAPTER 1
EARLY DAYS

'Get down off that table, NOW, or I'll tan your backside. Just wait 'til your mother gets home, you little bugger.' These are the very first words I can remember being spoke or shouted to me.

Cousin David and myself, I must have been about 3 or 4 years old – Dave was about 4 years older – were playing at something called 'Commando's which meant doing dangerous things like jumping from the highest stair before doing yourself any damage, or in this instance, launching yourself off the dining table onto a pile of stacked-up cushions in the middle of the floor. Dave had already landed and bounced off the cushions and smacked his head on the side of the fireplace which later resulted in a most impressive bruise. I was poised, counting down from ten – ten, 8, 7, 3, 5, 2, 1 'Go' - just about to push myself off from the drop-leaf table with the blood curdling cry of 'Commando' when in walked Grandma in her ankle length pinny overall, headsquare and carrying a bag. She had just been over the street to lay out a neighbour who had just croaked it. Old Alf, who lived directly opposite us in Mercer Street, had been badly for a long time. He lived with his younger brother, Dick, and must have been in his 80s at least.

Dick wouldn't allow anyone to take Alf away to hospital as he looked after his brother himself, or tried to. I just about remember playing out in the street and running (we always ran everywhere) past Dick's house and seeing Alf propped up in bed against the parlour window, he always had a blanket around his scrawny shoulders and a bobcap on which had been knitted for him by a neighbour. We always gave him a wave, giving back a toothless smile and raised a weary hand. Occasionally, Grandma would take across a dish of hotpot she had made for the two brothers and I would accompany her with the pudding wrapped up in a towel to keep it warm. On seeing us cross the street, he would wave and gesture to Dick to let us in. By the time we got in, Alf was sporting a set of teeth that didn't fit properly. When he tried to speak, they would clatter because they didn't fit, his gums had shrunk. I later found out they weren't his teeth but someone else's and they lived beside the bed in a tumbler of water on a little stool. There was a faded picture of Alf and Dick with their mum next to it, no sign of dad. It was, as I recall, freezing cold in there. They never lit a fire and of course, central heating was unheard of. Granddad would sometimes go across and light a fire for them on really cold nights and take a bucket of coal for them to keep it going, but they never did. The bucket of coal was still there on his next visit unused.

Mum arrived home from the mill about an hour after grandma had told us off and she grassed us up. 'I'll give you a whizzer if you do that again. You'll break your bloody neck.' Such was the bollocking I began to bubble a bit (always a good ploy for getting sympathy). Mum pulled me to her for a nice hug and a kiss on the head, 'Now, be a good lad.' All was well again as grandma prepared tea. Conversation between them changed from my death-defying stunts to old Alf. Mum said she would go around the neighbours to try and get a bit of a collection, not for flowers, but for Dick to help him out a bit. Food in your belly is better than a dying flower. My mum couldn't get time out from the mill for the funeral, so grandma went instead. She loaned me out to Mr Booth who had a small grocer's shop at the top of the street while she attended. He gave me a job of scattering sawdust on the tile floor of the shop. I then spent ages drawing in it with my finger, getting under the feet of the customers. He had a cat called Biscuit who was always in the window. I'm sure it used to cook when the sun shone. I was duly collected from Mr Booth on grandma's return.

After the funeral, all the neighbours started to open their curtains again as they all used to close them in those days as a mark of respect. But Dick's remained almost closed: only a slight gap was visible. They stayed like that always, in fact, I don't remember them ever being opened and I can't recall ever seeing Dick again. I remember granddad saying that he had 'taken bad ways'. He kept knocking on his door, but there was never an answer. Then one day, I saw some people gathered around the open front door and the curtains open. All the kids from the street wanted to look inside just to be nosey, but of course, were told to clear off.

What happened to him still remains a mystery to me, but someone did say that he died of something called a broken heart. The house became empty for ages, it seemed, and because no-one lived there, all the kids used the back yard as a den. You could just walk in the yard, because it had no gate, so the old shed became a meeting place for all the young scalleywags.

I was in there one time and Cyril, a lad that lived in Osborne Street, just around the corner, came in. He was very excited. He had nicked a fag from home and said he was going to smoke it, but couldn't: he had forgotten to nick a match to light it with.

Well, because I was the youngest in there and I was only across the from my own house, I was told to go home and flog a match from the kitchen. Off I went on my thieving trip only to find grandma in the kitchen. Making an excuse that I had come home for a drink. It was impossible to get a match from the kitchen, but spied a box on top of my mother's fags that were on top of the fireplace. If I had messed about trying to take just one match I would have been spotted, so I nicked the boxful instead. Rushing back with the box of matches, Cyril took them and struck one then lit the fag. He tried to look tough, but it nearly killed him. Some of the others in the shed tried to have a

3

drag of the ciggie, but I didn't. The ones that did were coughing and spluttering. Anyway, we all left the shed arranging to play footy after tea. I managed to put the box of matches back before mother came home from work. I felt like a hero, my place in the Mercer St gang was blossoming. I was only about 5.

Mother used to arrive home about 6pm from working at Cliff spinning mill: a fag and a brew was always the first thing she did on arriving, followed by long conversations on who did what and when with grandma. In between then and when granddad got home at about 7pm, I was allowed a snack, but, 'Not too much, or it will spoil your tea.' I was given half a slice of bread which I used to take to the scullery door, which was a space under the stairs. On the back of the door was nailed a smoked kipper, this was changed on a regular basis: wiping the bread on it a couple of times gave the bread a delicious smokey taste. It really did taste good.

The scullery used to contain all kinds of home produced potions that grandma used to call 'cure alls'. There were bottles of snig oil that was made from eels that were then swimming in abundance in the local river. Granddad used to have an eel trap and brought some home occasionally. He stripped off the skin, this made the oil, and ate the eels chopped and friend. The snig oil was used mainly for earache. If you put a couple of drops of the black stuff in your ears, it did seem to work (I think) and was also good for removing built-up wax as well.

Also on the shelves were bottles of goose grease. Again a good home remedy for winter colds and chesty coughs. We always had a goose at Christmas that granddad brought, it was cooked and eaten and the resulting grease (there always seemed to be plenty of it) was collected, strained and then bottled. So if a chesty cough or cold took hold during winter, grandma would take a few spoonfuls of grease and melt it on a plate in front of the range and make a poultice by spreading it on a large piece of cloth and slapping it on your chest keeping it on with an elastic bandage. This was followed by covering that with an old vest or liberty bodice and a jumper: it used to heat up, but it stank a bit. I don't know if it really worked or not, but she used to swear by it.

On the shelf, there was always a stock of night lights which were small, dumpy candles. I used to have one in my bedroom at night and it used to last a couple of hours then go out. Can you imagine these days letting a 5-year-old going to bed with a naked flame next to the bed. But to me, at the time, it was very comforting watching a small, flickering flame. When we had run out of night lights, Grandma would bring in a tiny oil lamp with a glass chimney on top to use which would last a bit longer. When Mum came to bed (I used to sleep in the same room) and if I was still awake, she would tell me to get under the covers to allow her to get undressed in private. She would then say, 'Okay' and I would emerge to watch her put a gentle hand behind the glass funnel and blow out the flame and with a, 'Night, night, love,' I would drift off with the slight smell of an extinguished flame – a smell I still love today when a candle is blown out. To me, it is a very comforting aroma.

My job, once a week, was a trip to Mrs Owen's shop on New Hall Lane to fill a bottle with paraffin for the oil lamp. She had a corner shop out of another era. A large, clanging bell above the door made a right din on entering and the shop was always dark, except for a single bulb over the counter. A creaky, wooden floor and dusty shelves contained all sorts of fascinating stuff: moth balls, donkey stones, firewood, fly papers and, of all things, a small library. Mrs Owen was a tiny lady. She always wore a floor-length pinny, tiny crooked glasses and clogs. I would arrive with a pop bottle to be filled with paraffin. She would stick a funnel in it and draw off a can full from a tank behind the counter. A shaky hand would fill the bottle and the top screwed on, wiping the neck on her pinny. She always asked how Annie (my grandma) was and said she would bob down and see her sometime. I don't think she ever did.

Mrs Owen was a very kind, gentle lady who, so said Grandma, lost two fine sons during the war. She had a tiny picture of them in a locket she always wore around her neck. She kept the shop as long as she could before ill health took hold. Mr Seward had a small shop next door and he broke in one day, with the aid of a policeman, when she didn't answer. She was found dead in bed still wearing the locket. I don't think she had any family as only Grandma, Granddad and Mr Seward attended the funeral. The shop never reopened and was demolished around 1960.

The shelf also had a number of other first aid items in an old toffee tin in which was the most dreaded item of all – a bottle of iodine. This was used to put on cuts and grazes and it used to sting like hell. There was also a tin of soot from our chimney, collected when the local chimney sweep, Mr Riley, came. I used to love it when he came, it seemed most exciting. He would arrive on a bike balancing his brushes on his shoulder and a large carrier on the back contained hand brushes and a large sheet. He was a very small fella, very humble with an obvious Irish accent. He always wore clogs and stunk of soot. I used to help by clearing the mantelpiece of ornaments. These were a couple of WWI shells kept polished, a few horse brasses of Granddad's and a Westminster chime clock which took pride of place in the middle. The ornaments on the hearth consisted of a couple of empty vases and a jug.

Mr Riley would make sure everything was cleared away including the peg rug and proceeded to fasten the cloth on top of the fireplace with bricks. Everyone always had a few bricks in their yard for such an event. A large chimney brush was held behind a small hole in the sheet and the first rod was screwed to it from the front, it was then shoved and began its journey up the flue screwing more and more rods as it progressed. At about halfway, he would pull it down again releasing a "boomf" of soot that hit the sheet. Again it was thrust upwards until it came out of the chimney top. I was then sent on a very important mission, to go across the street and shout, 'It's come,' when the brush appeared out of the chimney. I would watch it disappear as it was pulled back down again, rushing in to hear another "boomf" as more soot dropped. A couple more shoves up and down with the brush and the job was complete. He carefully unscrewed the brush and took it out of the front door and spun it to remove any dust. Grandma would make him a cup of tea and a customary half-hour wait to let the soot settle before removing the sheet was a chance for a good gossip with Mr Riley. He knew everything, as he used to visit everyone in turn. He knew more local news than the Lancashire Evening Post.

'Have you heard about Nellie from number 40?' or 'What about Mrs Clayton's fancy fella, then?' The news came thick and fast and Grandma gave him a few more bits of tittle tattle to take to his next customer. With the bricks removed from the mantelpiece, the soot ball was bundled carefully up and tied with a rope. The rods were wiped down and fastened together with a couple of leather straps. The soot ball was invaded by Grandma as she filled a tin with it and put in the scullery. Mr Riley then slung the bag of soot on his back while leaving his brushes in our back yard. He then pedalled to the local allotment site at Fishwick plots, about a ten minute ride away. They would pay him a bob or so for it, as it made a good greenfly spray and soil conditioner.

On returning to retrieve his rods and brushes, Grandma would pay him and off he went. He worked most of the streets in the vicinity and was never out of work. All the kids loved him and so did the mums as he was always in the know of some scandal or other. The tin of soot on the scullery shelf used to have another function besides aphid spray and soil conditioner. Granddad and Grandma used it to clean their teeth with. Granddad still had his own, but Grandma's were false. He used to wet a toothbrush and dab in the tin and clean his teeth with it. He looked like he had been sucking liquorice, but on rinsing his teeth became pearly white. Grandma cleaned hers by taking them out and scrubbing them in sooty water followed by a quick rinse, then put them back in again. I liked to ask her to smile at me when she had no teeth in. She looked funny and made me laugh.

The shelf also held an old snip tin, or butty tin, of Granddad's. It had a broken hinge and was held together with a large, elastic band. The tin was full of buttons of all shapes and sizes that Grandma collected, not only from our old clothes, but from her part-time job cleaning at the Plaza cinema. Any odd coins that were found, she gave to me to put in my money box. She would take me to school at St Matthews, then go cleaning until dinner time, pick me up for dinner and take me back again at 1.30pm. I used to get many treats off Grandma, any odd coins that she found she would give to me and I'm sure she gave me the odd penny or two from her own purse sometimes.

At the back of the scullery was a collection of bundles of firewood and a stack of briquettes for burning. These were lumps of compressed coal dust formed into bricks. They were cheaper than coal, but burned quicker. The coal man used to come to deliver a few bags. Mr Jed Billington came up the side lobby with a hundredweight of coal on his back and dumped it in the coal hole. Grandma used to watch him like a hawk. 'If I've paid for a bag, that's what I want. Not half of one.' Granddad always got on well with Jed because he had a horse that pulled the coal cart and Granddad was a horse man. In his younger days, he had his own horse when he worked on the canals around Preston. He was an orphan who was adopted by a family called the 'Baines' who ran a business from the canal basin in Preston. It's now filled in and a shopping complex containing Aldi and Poundland – a featureless looking place with a huge car park. Granddad used to visit Jed most weekends and talk "horses". I went with him on occasions to the stables which was 2 streets away. I was allowed to sit on the horse, it was called "Sovereign" or "Sov" for short. It was a big gentle beast, but I thought I was Roy Rodgers of the range. When a delivery took place and the kids were off school during holidays, Jed would allow us to ride on the cart with him. We never went far, only the local streets, as everyone had coal fires.

I once got into a bit of trouble and Jed had to "fill up again". He said, 'Do you want to come?' I straight away said, 'Yes please.' We went to the local coal yard about half an hour away and watched him fill the empty sacks by weighing each one on a scale then throwing them onto the cart. I pestered him to let me help fill the bags. He allowed me to do one or two, but I was too slow, so he took over. Unfortunately, I must have got more coal dust on me than was in the bags. On reaching home after about an hour and a half, Mum went berserk. 'Look at the state of him.' I got blamed for not telling her where I was going, but Jed also got a bollocking for bringing me back looking like Al Jolson.

One weekend at the stable, Granddad and Jed were talking about re-roofing the stable before winter set in. The horse would have to be moved out for a couple of days in order for the repair to be done. Granddad said he would look after it while the roof was renewed. I vividly remember coming home from school at the end of the week by Grandma and she said, 'Don't go into the lobby,' a shared access path that went up between our house and Mrs Lancaster's house next door. Sure enough, there was Sov pacing up and down in the lobby having a look over the yard gate and turning around to walk back again. It couldn't turn around in the lobby, it was too narrow. Grandma said, 'If that horse isn't out by Monday, it'll be in a stew.' I knew she was only joking as she would not have had anywhere to peg the washing out if it rained.

Throughout the weekend, all the gang came round to see the horse, feeding it bits of apple and carrots. I think it enjoyed the attention and was well petted. It had a bag of straw stuff and a bucket of water near the gate. It certainly didn't go hungry. When I was in the house, I would hear it clip clopping up and down. By Sunday night, Sov was ready to be taken back to its stable, so me and Granddad led him carefully back to his new roofed home. On returning, Grandma had a few words to say to Granddad, 'If you think I'm cleaning all that shit up, you've got another think coming.' So Granddad and I swept it up and washed it down, giving the manure to my Uncle Eddie who lived next door to us opposite to Mrs Lancaster. Uncle Ed must have had a good crop of spuds the year after from his makeshift potato bed in his back yard.

MERCER STREET

Dolly tubs and possers and a mangle in't yard,
Washboards and a big metal pail,
Whitewashed walls and dolly blue,
A bath on a 6 inch nail.

Lavvy on't top of a washed flag yard,
Wooden seat scrubbed till it was white,
Pieces of Evening Post on a string on't wall,
An oil lamp to use at night.

A shed with a bloomin' great lock on,
What wonders contained therein.
To see, I used to look through winda
By standing on a battered ol' bin.

Slopstone in kitchen an' only one tap
And coal 'ole under stairs,
A peg rug in front of a black leaded range,
Two or 3 odd comfy chairs.

No telly, but a big brown radio
With ornate front and big knobs.
A roaring fire and warm pyjamas
Laid out on a pile of logs.

No fridge, no freezer, but we ate well.
Stews and hotpots we came to no fault
On the table fresh bread and patted butter,
Homemade pickles and a dish of cob salt.

On't back door a big leather strap
For grandad to sharpen his razor.
And beside it, a hook with my name on
Onto which I hung my school blazer.

Snow used to last weeks and weeks
Playin' out till I couldn't feel my feet.
These and more memories come into my head
When I think of Mercer Street.

CHAPTER 2
STREET GAMES, AUNTIES AND UNCLES

Christmas in Mercer Street was always a good time. We certainly didn't have a lot of money, but somehow never went short of anything. Mum used to save in Aunty Mary's Christmas club, a bit a week, bought a few treats and presents. I always got an annual, either *Dandy* or *Beano* and a main present: a toy fort, a boxful of cowboys and Indians, a cowboy set with a Stetson hat with sheriff's badge on it, a holster and two pistols were amongst some I remember. My Christmas stocking usually contained an apple and orange, a little Dinky car and some crayons, wrapped in a mini stocking was a few pennies to spend. I was a millionaire.

As soon as the paper shop opened on New Hall Lane around the corner, I spent the money on a few packets of caps. These were tapes of about 18in long with little pinches of explosive powder on, all rolled up in a small round cardboard box. These were inserted into the body of my six-shooters, a cog fed the tape into the area for the hammer to strike every time you pulled the trigger and made a fabulous bang, even a bit of smoke used to come off as well. I felt 6ft tall wearing my weaponry. I'd shoot cats on the back yard wall, jump out at Mum and shoot her as well. No one got past "six gun Ramps" without being shot. I felt dangerous.

One of my friends, Graham, also had a toy gun that worked with caps. He had the brilliant idea of taking out all the pinches of explosive powder from the tapes and collecting it together. There must have been at least 20 or 30 pinches on a tape. These were collected and stuck onto a small piece of sticky tape and inserted behind the hammer of the gun. He had the idea of us both doing this, then have a fast draw and make a BIG bang and kill each other. Word got around that there was going to be a "shooting". So armed with our super explosive pistols and dressed in our finest cowboy gear, we had a small audience. A few practices of quick drawing saw us then face each other. Legs slightly apart, poised and ready just like we had seen at the pictures, tension was high. Even Graham's mum came to watch. We both drew and fired. After a few go's, mine went off with a loud bang, but Graham's didn't. His ammo had fallen off – I won. It was fun for about three seconds, but realised my pocket money for that week had disappeared in a puff of smoke. An expensive, but fun mistake.

Pester, pester, pester that's all I did for more ammo money – 3d a box, very expensive. Mum refused most of the time, but Granddad used to spoil me rotten sometimes. One night, on his return from work, he brought me a box full of 12 rolls of caps. Mum took some off me saying to use them carefully. No chance. By this time, all the Mercer Street gang had toy guns. Some had bows and arrows with suckers on the end. At the end of a gunfight one day, as we all sat around the street lamp, Alistair had another bright idea. If you take the sucker off the arrow and stick a needle on the end, it would stick into stuff. And so, an instant competition was born. Someone drew a target on Mr Bright's garage door and the arrow was converted. We took it in turns to hit bulls eye. With one eye shut, tongue stuck out at one side, dithering with the strain on the bow, I let fly. I hit the target a bit wide and the needle stuck in, but the arrow fell off. Our antics were soon spotted by a neighbour and stopped. 'You'll poke some bugger's eye out with that. Clear off.' It was great fun, but I must admit, it was a bit dangerous. Anyway, back to battle.

There seemed to be more fun in anything the gang did if it involved a bit of danger. We used to get a chap round occasionally collecting old clothes and rags, 'Rag and bone bods here again.' Grandma always had a few items she should couldn't mend anymore and she would get a few bob for them, depending on the weight. She once threw out an old pair of pants of mine that were too small anyway, along with a busted pair of braces that held them up. The braces were ok, but the leather bit with the button hole in it was missing. I managed to retrieve the braces before they got given away. It was an idea I had for a while. At the bottom of Mercer Street, there was a factory lodge which served to cool the machinery in the local mill. It was surrounded by a spiked top metal fence. I don't know what the spikes were to achieve, as you could bend the bars and squeeze through. At the far side of the lodge, there was a couple of railings missing. They were never repaired considering it was a dangerous place. So a few of us had the idea of making a massive catapult from my old braces and fastened the ends to the railings on either side of the gap. At the point where the back brace met the front was a patch of leather that would act as a pouch and you get a big strain on the elastic straps. But what about ammo? Searching the banks of the lodge, we found plenty of stones. Unfortunately, we couldn't fire anything large as the pouch wasn't big enough. Again, taking it in turns to fire a stone as far as we could across the lodge resulted in stiff competition. We even got an audience of kids from William Henry Street along, but I don't think they were too impressed. They were a bit posher than us and most of them had bikes. The braces soon gave up the ghost and after several attempts at repairs, they were whizzed into the lodge.

Playing faggies got quite competitive. We would scout the streets, especially the bus stop bin, for empty cigarette packets. The more variety of packets meant we got the better the collection. The ciggie packets then were like match boxes, the outer sleeve could be flattened into a card. They were not the flip top efforts of today. The game involved each player placing 2 or 3 packets up against the wall and pavement. Each player took it in turn to flick a "faggie" to try and knock down one that was standing up. If you succeeded, you took the ones knocked down as well as your own. This continued until you missed. The last card standing would be claimed by the "chucker" as well as any miss throws. It was all very confusing and many arguments were heard, accusing each other of getting too close, or the wind blew it down. With a bit more thought and sponsorship, it could have been an Olympic sport.

While collecting the "faggies", we would also collect used bus tickets, but only certain ones. They used to have serial numbers along the top and only the ones whose numbers totalled twenty-one were any good. Anyone who fancied a girl would give her a ticket, if she ripped it down through the numbers it was a sign to take a hike. If she ripped it the other way, leaving the numbers intact, you had a chance – at what, I don't know. It was always a chance to shout, 'You've got a girlfriend. You've got a girlfriend,' or 'Loseeeer, Loseeeer.'

Graham, who lived at the bottom of the street with his sister, Margaret, was our local millionaire. He had a massive bag of marbles or "allys" as we called them. I don't know where he got them from, but he had hundreds. All I seemed to have was a handful. My collection never made it to Graham's hoard. Everyone had a few, they could be bought from Mr Wallen's paper shop for 3d a bag. In the pavements there were several "puggyholes" – bits of flags broken at the corner with a piece missing. Digging out a bit of muck from that made a hole – a target to get a hole in one. If you missed the hole and your opponent "holed" then you lost your marble to him or her. Little Peter once got into a fight with Graham accusing him of getting too close to the puggyhole. Little Peter lost his marbles "literally" and bashed him one. It got as far as their mums coming out to sort out the mess, but after a day of sulking, they were all friends again.

At the near top of Mercer Street was a garage that belong to Mr Bright who kept a wagon in it. It was a garage with an upstair's store room – he just collected junk really. It was a dirty, dusty place that was full of nooks and crannies, just the place for playing army. The weapon of choice for playing in there was a peashooter. Mr Bright let us play in there whenever he was around and tinkering with the engine. He always used to say, 'Well, kids have to play.' A visit to Mr Booth's shop for a bag of pigeon peas, which were often bought by taking back empty pop bottles getting 1d for each bottle, saw us ready and armed for another battle. Running silly around, under and in the wagon, upstairs, downstairs, hiding, making dens and shooting through a broken window was great fun, even if you did get a pea in the eye from a well-aimed sniper. Running out of peas saw us searching on the floor for used ones, or even better, the odd ball bearing that was knocking about. It's funny that no-one lost an eye or swallowed a ball bearing before it was fired. The garage, unfortunately, burned down not long after. Watching the firemen was exciting, but tragically, we lost our theatre of war.

Everything we did was always physical and done at breakneck speed. Chasing, tig, underarm relieve O, under leg relieve O – the latter was particularly brill if the girls came to play as well. It involved someone being "on" and they had to run and try to tig someone else – just touch them. If they caught you, you had to stand legs apart until someone else relieved you by crawling between your legs. The girls always scrunched up their skirts and tucked them under their knickers, resulting in a load of screams and occasional slap from some reliever who went a bit too far. It was a case of the more the merrier in this game. If a large gang gathered, two tiggers would chase the rest hoping to get everyone legs astride to win.

My aunt and uncle lived next door to us as well and they both worked. She worked at Cliff cotton mill and my uncle worked at Post Office telephones. Cousin George, their son, also worked – he was at George Moss bike shop on New Hall Lane. On occasions, my aunt used to brag a bit about what they could afford. Once it was a television, then a radiogram, then this, then that. Uncle Ed was a very handy fella, making things didn't seem any bother to him. He made a sort of fitted kitchen, not the type you see today, but everything under a worktop with proper cupboards and a built-in sink. Aunty asked us round to view the big unveiling, so off we went. Mum was very envious as Aunty stood there purring, but Grandma would have none of it. She had a classic response saying, 'Well, Mary, you can have all the fancy kitchens you want, it won't make you a better cook.' Speechless. I think that rings true today as well. Some of these kitchens look more like clinical operating theatres with a strategically placed piece of fruit on the worktop for effect and some model or other holding a glass of wine. Grandma's kitchen was less than basic, but each day she produced the world's best food. God bless her.

Grandma's brother, Mum used to call him Uncle Joe, came to see us on occasions. A very tall, smartly dressed chap. Gran and Granddad had a lot of time for him and made a fuss. What I was told at the time, I didn't understand and was told not to stare at him as he had a habit of pulling funny faces. It seemed his eyes used to open really wide and his jaw would drop open at any time. Grandma always made him a cup of tea and a piece of cake. He would hold the cup, that was only made half full, with very shaky hands. After taking a drink, he would sort of pant a bit. I got used to seeing him and it didn't bother me much. Mum said it was a shame for him as she told me he still suffered from something called shell shock from his military service during World War I. Visiting his home in Annis Street further down the lane, it was full of army memorabilia and plenty of photos of him in uniform. One was of him holding what looked like a long flag astride a horse. This very proud photo sat in a big frame over the fireplace. When his wife died, he hardly came to see us anymore and Grandma said he wasn't looking after himself. He, too, passed away shortly after his wife, Only 4 people went to his funeral at the cemetery. Two of them was Grandma and Granddad.

There used to be a shelter at the bottom of the lane where, during the day, all the old fellas would meet for an hour or two to have a smoke and a natter about the old days. This was usually after the pub across the road, "The Rose Bud", closed at 3.30pm. They would meet in there most days prior to going their separate ways for tea, but not before they all visited the iron duke – a black metal toilet block in the middle of the road. Evenings would see them returning just in time for the pub opening up again at 6pm. When they disappeared, the lads and me would take their place armed with note pads and collecting car numbers. Why? Because we did.

Buses and wagons had their own column, it was a good place to collect as it was the main road south out of Preston. It was before motorways were built. We would cop Standerwick white ladies, old-type charabangs as well as Corporation buses, Panthers and Tigers. Next to the shelter was Tyron's motorcycle shop. We would drool over what bike we would buy when we grow up. Some of the bikes were second-hand, so we would get their numbers as well.

All life used to surround the shelter. One Saturday evening, it started to chuck it down, so playing out was a no, no. We hot-footed it to the shelter to find a fella and woman having a snog. We all piled in, much to their disgust. They cleared off into the pub across the road. Not too long after, a woman came marching down the lane holding a plate. She had a face like thunder. She stood at the vault window and banged on it shouting someone's name. Nothing happened, but proceedings caught all of our attention. She started screaming and shouting at the pub door, obviously something didn't suit. The inner door opened and a chap appeared. She let him have the plate, complete with a dollop of food on it, straight into him, then marched off. He stood their brushing the best he could. Leaning out of the door, he gave her a mouthful. She stopped, turned and gave him some back. The door slammed and she strode off and peace returned. That's what's called entertainment.

Entertainment came in all kinds of guises, pigeon catching was one where we would all sit really quiet and still. As one lad brought a slice of bread and would flick a piece or two onto the pavement. Pigeons would soon arrive and venture ever closer. A couple more bits of bread onto the shelter step would see the capturer try and chuck a jacket over it. Most times, it missed, but on occasion there was success. They would flap like mad under the coat, 'Got it, got it.' It would always be release afterwards though.

The Rose Bud pub had a large dartboard painted on the wall outside, presumably letting people know that a dartboard was on offer inside. This also became an instant game for us as on a hot day, the tar would melt between the stone sets in the road. This could be picked off and rolled into sticky balls. A tiny bit stuck gently into the end of a peashooter, followed by a massive blow would let the blob splat against the dartboard. Again, massive fun, cost nowt and hurt no one. Great.

Next to Philip's chippy, there was a paper shop that at tea time a few bigger lads would gather with big bags ready to deliver the Evening Post. Some smaller lads, including myself, would offer to help them in the hope of a few pence at the end of the week. The lads would deliver piles of papers and would sometimes return for a second run after filling up again. I would help carry the bag and deliver some, but it was a bit too far away for me, especially at tea time as I latched myself onto a more local shop in the lane, Mr Wallen's. I helped a mate deliver some down our street. Seeing some mates playing footy, I decided to ditch the job and joined in. The ball went over a back yard wall and a fella by the name of Ol' Caton lived there. I don't know if this was his name or not, but that's what he was known as. Knocking on the door to get the ball back brought no response, but a very loud and angry bark from Caton's dog, a great beast of a thing. I think it was a cross between a lion and something prehistoric. I rushed home to get my ball and the game continued. Again the ball disappeared over his wall. The dog, by this time, was in the back yard – he had obviously let it out. It was going mental. I knocked on the door, but there was no response, so went home and told Granddad.

'Oh no, not him,' he said. 'He's a nasty piece of work. Worse than his bloody dog.'

Granddad went to knock on his door, but again there was no response. He shouted, 'Jack, Jack, it's George,' and banged again. The door opened slightly and he said, 'Come any more and I'll set the dog on you.' Granddad replied, 'Look, give the lad his ball back or I'll kill your dog.' This was getting heavy! The door slammed shut. Back home, Grandma said that Caton and Granddad never got on. Anyway, a couple of days later, a policeman came to the door with Ol' Caton, accusing Granddad of killing his dog. They had no proof and things went quiet.

Quite a while later, when Ol' Caton moved, I found out he did kill his dog by soaking a lump of sponge in gravy and throwing it over the yard wall. Of course, the dog choked on it and croaked. But I never got my ball back. Cross Granddad at your peril.

Once a week, usually a Friday, he would go to the New Hall Lane tavern up on the lane and bring a jug of beer home. He would fill his pint cup and enjoy it listening to the radio. I asked what it tasted like and he offered me a sip from an egg cup. Yuck, it was horrible. He told me it would put hairs on my chest. I'm still waiting and I'm sixty-eight now. I keep trying.

MARGARET BLACKWELL AT 7

It would be about 1954 or 5
I had two friends that were swell
One was Bobby Fletcher from topo' street
At the bottom was Margaret Blackwell.

Bobby was alright, but he had eczema
And was always scratchin' hisself
So when he wasn't playing out, I'd play instead
With my friend Margaret Blackwell

We used to have many adventures
During summers that were long and hot
Playing doctors and nurses and marbles
Picnics with jam butties and pop.

I had a lot of things in common
With the best friend I ever had
Like wearing national health glasses
No brother's, no sisters, no dad.

We collected stones and used bus tickets
Daisies and dandelion tops
In those lovely innocent days of long ago
Which I hoped would never stop.

I remember she once made a backpack
Out of a box and some string
Then went for a walk to Waverley park
To play on't slide and swings.

On the way I asked her what's in it
She said it was Jesse, her dolly
A comb, a hairband and a handkerchief
And a half chewed sticky red lolly.

We got to the park and the swings were full
Then Arthur arrived on his new trolley
Showing off what his dad had made him
Maggie ignored him, then gave me her lolly.

Arthur was getting real miffed off
And went away not getting a date
We then played on't slide then went home
Just me and Maggie, my mate.

I sucked the lolly all the way home
Bragging with a party trick
Hopping on one leg from one lamppost to the next
Then I gave her back the stick.

We got back tut street and she had to go in
Said she would play out after tea
So I called for her on my wonky bike
Then played, just Maggie and me.

Maggie's mum called her, it was time for bed
We'd had a full day of games of fun
And looked forward with not a care in the world
For tomorrow was for more play in the sun.

Time moved on and she moved away.
She'll now be sixty-three
Occasionally I think of her
I wonder if she thinks of me.

CHAPTER 3
GRANDDAD AND SCHOOL HOLIDAYS

Once a fortnight or so, Granddad would cut and chop firewood. He used to bring lumps of wood home from work and sort them out at a later date. He took immense pride in the tools he had – the rip saw was always cleaned and sharpened and oiled after each use. All other tools were neatly stacked in drawers in the shed. I sort of helped by gathering the sticks and taking them in to Grandma who put them neatly by the side of the fireplace to dry properly. I could only go in the shed when Granddad was there, because there were some sharp tools inside and he didn't want me to come out minus a few fingers as Mum would be vexed.

But one day, he did leave me. 'I won't be a minute, don't touch anything.' Freedom! I managed to get a box off the top shelf. It felt funny, all waxy feeling with a long strap on it. Well, I had to have a look inside. I'd got this far. In it was a kind of face mask and a long thing sticking out in front. Granddad returned and said I'd been rummaging. He told me it was a gas mask and let me try it on. It stunk of rubber and I couldn't see through the visor. The end unscrewed off the sticky-out bit and that's where the filter was. I decided to scare Mum with it. Feeling my way back to the house, I ran in with a, 'Woo, woo, woo.'

'Oh, my God. Who's this?'

I wanted to play out with it, but wasn't allowed. It was returned to its shelf, never to be enjoyed again.

A great big vice was bolted on to the bench in the shed. I used to put my fingers in it and fasten it up slowly to see what it felt like. It bloody hurt! Cousin Dave's dad also had a vice in his shed, but he had better access than what I had. Many times we would torture each other for laughs, doing the same trick. On day, I found myself alone in our own shed, 'Now what can I make?' I fastened a lump of wood in the vice and proceeded to bash a big nail into it. It just about held and followed it with a swinging blow from a big hammer. The nail flew off like a bullet and cracked the window. 'Oh, no! I'm going to die!' I wasn't allowed in that shed again without Mum or Granddad. My construction of a lump of wood with a big nail in it never made it off the ground.

School holidays during the summer used to last 6 weeks. Mum used to have 2 weeks holidays from the mill. These 2 weeks with Mum were terrific. She purchased British Rail runabout tickets from Frames travel agent in town. I think it was for £5. These tickets could take you by train to all the local seaside resorts – Blackpool, Southport, Morecambe and Fleetwood – but the best trip by far was to Windermere. Not only could we go to Lakeside, but we could also travel on the Windermere ferries as they were also run by British Rail. A trip from Lakeside took us to Bowness, then on to Ambleside. Once, Granddad came along as well. When we arrived at Ambleside, he would pay for us to go out on the lake on a rowing boat. We would take our butties with us to have on the lake, giving Mum a peaceful hour on shore to have an ice cream. The return journey to Lakeside to catch the last train home saw me visit the souvenir shop to spend the money Grandma had given me.

Fleetwood was a good trip too. It was a tradition that me and Mum had fish and chips on arriving in the station cafe. She used to say this was the best chippy on earth because the fish came fresh every day from the trawlers that landed at Wyre dock which was just up the road. Mum had some friends who lived in Fleetwood, Bert and

Bessie. We stayed with them on occasions for a night. This gave me an opportunity to play at the boating lake. My spends were used on one occasion to buy a two-man submarine that worked by winding up an elastic band, putting it in the water and letting go. I let it go, but it didn't come back up, so I went back to Bessie's to get Mum, but Bert came and retrieved it for me. From then on it was confined to the bath only.

Blackpool was magical. I used to get really excited waiting at Preston station with bucket and spade watching a huge steam engine come in. Eyes were skinned to see who could spot Blackpool Tower the first. Again, holiday spends were on 1d slots and perhaps a bunch of paper flags on sticks that were stuck on top of my sandcastles. Jugs of tea could be bought on the prom to take to the beach, but nothing beat a double whopper with chocolate sauce and sit on a hired deckchair viewing my sandcastle kingdom. We had to use the runabout tickets every day to get our money's worth and they were well used. Mum's second week was mainly for rest, but that was the start of a few weeks of playing out in long, hot summer days. Rain or shine, it didn't make any difference. Every day was for inventive fun. I don't know where it came from, but someone found an old dolly tub. These were used for doing the weekly wash with a posser, a long brush handle with a wooden disc on the end that pummelled or 'possed' the washing in the tub. The dolly tub had a few holes in it, so it was useless for its intended use, but not to us. Taking it in turns, someone would get inside, squeeze your back on one side and brace yourself on knees and hands. This was rolled along Birley Bank an adjacent road from one end to the other being bashed by the runners. Getting out saw the volunteer victim completely dizzy and half deaf. 'My turn, my turn', arguments as to who wanted to be half killed were often heard. Better than any fairground ride and cheaper.

Granddad seemed to have a lot of time for me. He took me everywhere at weekends. He first introduced me to fishing back in the early 50s. A Ribble bus trip to Garstang with his sniptin full of butties, a flask of brew, a small box of fishing tackle and a rod made from an old tank aerial were the ingredients for a great adventure. It was the first time I caught my first fish – a tiny perch which I took home wrapped in the greaseproof paper that the butties were wrapped in. I wanted to show Mum and Grandma, as well as my friends, my prize. Grandma told me to chuck it in the bin, but I wanted to keep it. So when Granddad was putting the tackle back in the shed, I nailed it to the shed wall, thinking it would stay like that. After an hour or two, it disappeared and confined to the bin before it started to pong. That first little outing, catching a tiny fish, set a seed in me. I'm still fishing sixty-three years later, but the tackle has been slightly upgraded. The lodge at the bottom of the street then became my regular fishing venue catching sticklebacks and tadpoles, jam jars full of things brought great pleasure. Although we were told it was a dangerous place, it didn't stop us having fun in there. Making rafts once and nearly drowning saw the riot act read to us. The mill owners began to repair the fences after a complaint and soon was locked out of bounds. Spoil sports.

It was about that time that Granddad started to become ill. He just used to sit at home instead of taking me out at weekends. He would sit for hours, elbows on his knees, rubbing his head and staring into the fire. Grandma said, 'He keeps remembering things,' and would sometimes just go to bed through the day. We always had the radio on and one night, he was sitting in his usual place, I vividly remember a particular song came on, it was 'Danny boy, the pipes are calling'. Granddad burst into tears, sobbing quietly. I was puzzled and upset at seeing him like this, so Mum and Grandma took me next door to Aunt Mary's while they put him to bed and called the doctor. Poor Granddad didn't get any better. Mum was always running up and down stairs and Grandma did what she could. They transferred his bed down to the parlour to save time running upstairs. Dr Pimlott came a few times, but one night after he had gone, Granddad had a stroke.

Mum went to Mrs Exleys a couple of doors down to ring up and he was taken away. He was returned quite a while later, but he looked so different. His face had changed and he never spoke. All he could do was shout things I didn't understand. It was sort of frightening for me. Playing out in the street, I could see him in the parlour. It reminded me of seeing Alf, who used to live across the road.

It would take Mum and Grandma ages to settle him down at night, but sometimes I could hear him shout out. I just laid in bed and could hear Grandma going downstairs. Things got worse and he was taken away. I asked where he had been taken. They told me he was in a safe placed called Whittingham Hospital. I later found out it was a mental institution. There he spent many years, Mum visiting him every Saturday afternoon. Uncle George, Dave's dad, took her and me in his Ford Popular car, but I wasn't allowed to see him, I stayed in the car with Uncle George. Mum and Aunty Ethel came out many times with tears in their eyes, but put on a good face for me. I really missed having him around. At that age, I thought he would be with me forever. My first real lesson on this thing called life. We did have some wonderful times together. I still miss him.

He died on February 4th, 1963 aged seventy-four in Whittingham Hospital. The night was snowy and very cold as a telegram arrived telling us that he died at 6.10pm – we all cried. Mum, later on, went to bed as she was suffering with a bad cold. She shouted down to Grandma to come upstairs, as she did, they found that the alarm clock had stopped at the precise moment of his death. Grandma also had a clock, that too had stopped. Mum's watch, she found out the morning after, had also stopped at 6.10pm. The mantelpiece clock was still going. My Grandma said it was a sign to say that some things do stop, but a sign said life carries on. I didn't go to the funeral as I was at school then.

Life in Mercer Street carried on much as usual. I developed a bad skin condition at one time. The doctor sent me to hospital to have sunlamp treatment to improve my skin. I was to attend three times a week for a full twelve months. Mum and Grandma took it turns to take me. Grandma usually as Mum would have to take time out from the mill. After a month or two of this, I started to get a bit complacent. I had to lay on a bed with the lamps over me and turn every fifteen minutes. The treatment lasted an hour. Wearing dark glasses and having a card over my face got a bit boring, so I waited until the nurse in charge left me alone for a few minutes then took the card and glasses off and looked at the bright light, playing about blinking and seeing the light although my eyes were closed. I did this on several occasions – the result was that the bright spot didn't disappear. This concern led Mum to take me to the opticians. It was found I had burnt the back of my eye, irreparable damage, only slightly corrected by wearing national health glasses.

These were awful things, just glass and wire, it made me look simple, I hated them. Towards the end of junior school, one favourite prank was to see who could piss the highest up the toilet wall in the school toilets. The walls of the open-air urinal were great big slabs of slate with a pot gutter at the bottom and if you were clever and the slate was dry, you could draw on it or write your name. If you were in their by yourself, it was fun to run up and down drawing wavy lines and finish with a full stop. The pissing contest was fun, it didn't matter if you were good or not at lessons, all you needed between winning and losing was a full bladder and good piss pump.

I was going mad for a bike – a proper two-wheeled one. I used to enviously look in George Moss's shop window on New Hall Lane at all the racing bikes. I wish, I wish. For my birthday, Mum and Grandma bought me a second-hand one. It wasn't a racer, but a roadster. It was a bit big for me. I had to sit on the cross bar just to reach the pedals. It was hard to learn as the street was all cobbles, so I would fly down the pavement scraping my toes on the ground as I went. I was not very popular with Mum! But learn I did. It was life changing. I started to venture out and found a place called the Loney Hill. It had a rough path that led down to the river. It was very steep and full of pot holes. I used to ride down there with the brakes on dragging my feet as well. It was very exhilarating. Mum said not to let anybody else ride it as it could get stolen as that place had a few undesirables. After school one night, a friend, Colin, suggested we have a race down there. I was getting more competent by now and looked forward to the challenge. Graham came along as the starter. Off we went, Colin was well in the lead, I was dragging my feet, hit a pot hole and came off with a might crash. Not only did I buckle the front wheel, I obtained lots of cuts and grazes. Worst of all, I broke my glasses. Mum went barmy. I didn't have a spare pair of specs, so had to endure things out of focus for a few days while they were repaired. The bike was repaired as well at George Moss's shop and I was threatened to have the bike confiscated if that happened again. I held onto that bike for years, gradually growing into it only to have it completely wrecked in a crash.

To help protect my knees, they were always adorned by Elastoplast plasters. Mum thought I should be trying long trousers by now. Cousin Dave's mum was throwing a pair of his out, so I tried them on. Held up by a pair of braces, they weren't a bad fit, but a lot too long. Instead of cutting them shorter and hemming them, they were turned up on the inside and stitched. 'They will do for playing out in.' So now wearing protective clothing, I was set. I was getting quite used to having long pants on. I would change into them on arriving home from school, saving my short pants for better. It wasn't long before I was in "longs" permanently. I felt grown up, although they were a itchy.

Getting my hair cut was not a good experience for me. Every 3 or 4 weeks or so, I would be sent to Mr Miller's barber shop at the corner of Mercer Street and New Hall Lane. It was always a Friday evening to get my hair cut to make me tidy for the weekend. His shop was very grim, all gloomy and stinking of pipe smoke. On entering, there was a bell hanging against the door that clanged when the door opened and closed. A single torture chair sat in front of a mirror waiting for its next victim. Mr Miller would enter the shop from the back through a green curtain and put the light on. He was a very tall fella with a bad limp and always smoking a pipe. 'With you in a minute,' as he disappeared to bring back a pint pot of tea, the insides of which was as brown as the shop walls. He would place a small plank across the arms of the chair and began, never asking how you wanted it, everyone had the same. Grandma always told me to tell him to, 'Take plenty off. Get your money's worth.' If I would have said that, he would have skinned me. Besides being very rough, he constantly had his pipe stoked up blowing clouds of smoke all over the place. After the haircut, I'd pay and he would disappear behind the green curtain again.

Each Saturday, Mum would take me to town to do a bit of shopping, always visiting a cafe for a brew or a hot orange. A visit to "Woollies" for bits of stuff and I always got to buy a toy soldier for my collection, or a cowboy or Indian. A new figure would always take pride of place on the rug in front of the fire as soldiers battled both cowboys and Indians around hides made out of stacked up dominoes or cardboard boxes. A couple of toy boats always had a battle in the bath with figures being killed or drowned. The bath was always hung on a big nail that was bashed into the wall in the back yard. Every Friday night, we would bring it in to let it warm in front of the fire before filling it with buckets of hot water that we got from the free-standing gas boiler in the kitchen. I was to play upstairs while Mum had a bath, being called down when she had finished. I wasn't allowed in the bath first in case I had a wee in it. It was then my turn, a top up of hot water and a bar of carbolic or coal tar soap was administered. After washing, I could play in the bath until it went cool, having naval battles with all sorts of ships, some made from match boxes, but these soon went mushy. Plastic soap trays were good, firing at them with a water pistol until they filled and sank. A bit of devilment saw me firing into the open fire that was a couple of feet away when Mum wasn't watching, resulting in a long hissing sound. Ginger, our cat, used to get a blast as well if it ventured anywhere near. The bath was emptied by bucket and a ladling can into the drain outside until the bath was almost empty. You couldn't get the last bit out, so it was carried out and upturned into the drain, or "suff" as Grandma called it, then hung back on its nail again.

Freshly washed, we would listen to the radio. On Friday night it would be Wilfred Pickles in a show called "Have a Go" with prizes given away to the winner. He would say to his assistant, 'What's on the table, Mable?' and she would rhyme off all the exotic prizes, like an encyclopedia, or a set of cushions. I would stop up a bit later on Friday nights, because there would be no school next morning. Saturday morning, before going to town with Mum, I listened to "Children's Favourites" with Uncle Mac. His sign off would be, 'Goodbye children everywhere.' He played tunes like "Sparky's Magic Piano", "Little Sir Echo" and the "Troll Song". It was followed by the The Archie Andrews Show, a ventriloquist called Peter Brough was the main man. He was useless really, he got away with it on radio, but when he advanced to TV, he died a death. If Mum wasn't going to town for any reason, I would go to the local cinema, The Plaza. It's now a petrol station on the New Hall Lane. There was always a cartoon, usually *Tom and Jerry* followed by a cowboy film – *Hopalong Cassidy*, *Cisco Kid* and my favourite, *The Lone Ranger*. 'Hi Ho Silver!' Tea time was always a visit next door to Aunty Mary's to watch telly. They were the only ones in the street to own one. I would watch *The Bumblies* with Michael Bentine and my favourite *Billy Bunter* which was about a fat, greedy, public schoolboy who was always in trouble with Mr Welch, the headmaster. It wasn't long until we also got a telly. I don't think it was new as it had a few big marks on the wooden case, and the knobs were missing with just a metal peg onto which it should have sat. I wasn't allowed to watch too much, not that there was a lot on anyway, but "Sea Hunt" with a very young Lloyd Bridges was good, as was "Armand and Michaela Denis on Safari".

Around that time, Mum found herself a boyfriend. Eddie was a very kind man and we had many walks in Avenham and Miller parks. He had a son about my age and we would have hours of fun rolling down the slopes until we almost threw up. She was very happy with Eddie, but when Grandma found out, she forbade her to see him again. 'You're asking for trouble again, lady. Keep well away.' But I knew they continued to see each other for some time. Unfortunately, Eddie passed away from a heart attack, I think. Mum missed him terribly and so did I. She seemed to have lots of slanging matches with Grandma and was always crying. She had had enough of living with Grandma and Granddad that she decided to try and get a house of our own. She tried her best, but couldn't really afford it which made her feel worse. She became depressed and came out in rashes and lost some hair, but Grandma was very hard on her. I once told her to leave Mum alone. I received a good clout. But it all seemed to blow over in time and peace returned again. Life carried on as before.

CHAPTER 4
GROWING UP

A move to a slightly bigger house happened to be nearer my secondary school. I was to attend Fishwick County which was about fifteen minutes' walk away. After the move, or "flit" as Grandma called it, I never saw much of my friends from Mercer Street and never fitted in with the local lads because I was a little backward at coming forward with the new faces at our new street. Mum decided it a good idea if I was toughened up a bit, especially as I would have to have gone into the army, something called conscription when I came of age. Grandma agreed, 'Just what that lad needs. At least he'll have a decent haircut.' So they enrolled me into a judo class that met each Monday at Whitcliffe Memorial Church meeting room.

I arrived, but wasn't looking forward to it. Paying my subs, I was to attach myself to a young lad with all the gear – white suit, belt and a crew cut. He was a bit of a mini beast. After putting out all the mats, I was told to get changed. Well, all I had was an old pair of pants and an old shirt. I felt a bit of a dipstick as I also had to take off my glasses. I couldn't see a damn thing – blind as a bat. My young teacher was showing me the hold and how to fall properly without hurting myself. I fell alright, but it hurt. I didn't want to be there really and didn't enjoy it. Break time we had a drink of orange juice and watched a demo by the bigger lads. I thought, 'Sod this for a game of tiddlywinks, it's not in my line at all.' I told the main man I had to leave early making up an excuse. I never went back. Decades later, my wife told me that she had achieved the distinction of being a former judo champion. A martial arts expert and holding a second Dan black belt in karate. Just think, if I had the bottle to keep on with my fledgling judo career, we could have had fun knocking each other's blocks off, but it wasn't to be.

Talking of guns earlier, my mate Colin said he was going to buy one, 'Yeah right. What are you going to do? Go into the army stores and say, "Can I have a gun, please?"' Each week he would take his dinner money to school, but not give it in. He would go without any dinner and hide the money. A lad living in his street had an air rifle for sale, so Colin gave him his first week's dinner money as a deposit. He would pay each week until it was bought. He did manage it. He hid it from his mum and dad under his garden shed. Managing to sneak it out we met at the Loney Hill to shoot, but it didn't work. He tried to get his money back, but no chance so just ditched it.

Our next-door-neighbour, Mr Walton, helped at times to look after Grandma who was by that time not well. Mr Walton also took me fishing on occasions. One weekend, he and a friend took me to Glasson dock fishing. I was freezing cold, I didn't have much in the way of cold-weather clothes. I realised they took me for one reason – that was to look after the tackle once they had cast out, as they cleared off to the pub. Still, I enjoyed the outing and he would give me bits of tackle to start a collection – a bit of a carrot, I think, so that I would go with them again. He took me once to Arnside, it seemed such a long way. I had never been as far in my life, it was about 1½ hours away. It became a bit scary, because we literally had to run: the tide was coming in fast. I finished up getting a piggy-back back to the shore. When I told Mum what went on, she wouldn't let me go again with him. But by then, I had acquired a bit of fishing tackle and any bits that Granddad had become mine. I had enough to go on solo trips to the river. I would pester Mum to buy me a proper reel. I set my heart on an Intrepid Envoy – a fixed spool job that would be the bee's knees. But at 19s/11d, it was out of Mum's league, so I persevered with a wooden centre pin until times got better.

I got friendly with two local lads, Colin and David, who were also interested in fishing. Whenever we could, we would be down the river digging up worms and having rare old adventures. It was one summer during the school holidays, with our parents' permission, to spend a couple of days camping on the banks of the river. Colin had a small tent and some bits of equipment, and so off we went. All I took was a blanket and some butties with a tin of Ambrosia rice pudding. It was fine throughout the day, but when night came, it got bloody cold. Both Colin and Dave had sleeping bags and were okay, but I shivered under my blanket. We couldn't sleep, it was too much of an adventure, so we had a good laugh having farting competitions. When brewing up a ripper got hard work, who could do the loudest belch kept us amused. Early morning saw us dozing a bit, but we were suddenly awakened by something moving outside. A sort of shuffling sound and something touching the tent. We were all scared stiff. Who was going to undo the zip and find out? The shuffling became heavier and Dave said, 'Just open the zip and make a run for it.' So he undid it a little way to find a cow the size of Godzilla looking at him. It scared the cow as well as us as it backed off. There was a herd of the things all around us. We decided to stay put and they gradually moved off.

It was just coming light, we hadn't had much sleep belching and farting wasn't funny anymore, anyway it was breakfast time. We all had butties and I borrowed Colin's camping knife to open the tin of pudding. Giving myself a nasty gash with the cut tin, breakfast consisted of a butty and a blood-streaked rice pudding, cold and straight from the tin, washed down with a bottle of cold orange. The weather warmed up quite quickly once the sun came out, but during the afternoon, three bigger lads came along the bank and approached us. They insisted they wanted to use our tent to get changed in as they were going to swim slightly upriver where it was a bit more shallow.

We had no choice but agree. They left their clothes in the tent and disappeared. We checked inside after they had gone and found all our money, there wasn't much of it, had been stolen and found it in their pockets. A decision saw us retrieve our money and then proceeded to pack up in quick time. Tent down, gear packed, everything in about thirty minutes. Their clothes were just left in a heap on the river bank. Dave, giving them a good punchy kick before we left. We went our separate ways getting home. I was starving, so Grandma made an early tea. I'm not cut out for this camping lark. I slept well that night.

Adventure was always sought when playing out. One very dangerous place was the lime pits on a place called Fishwick View or "The Bonk" as it was called by us. No fencing, a steep hill ran from the bank down to 4 deep lime pits. These dirty white lakes kept us amused for ages, lobbing bricks, old tyres or anything else we could find into them. It would make a deep spudging noise and create a hole that gradually filled in with the liquid lime. That same summer, someone almost died in there and were only pulled out just in time. After that, the pits were filled in and fenced.

Dave, Colin and I would spend most of the school holidays together along with another lad, Philip, his dad had a chippy on London Road at the end of the lane. When we called for him during early evening, a free bag of chips was always on offer. Towards the end of the holidays, we would start to gather wood and any old crap that would burn ready to store away in Phil's back yard ready for bommie night. Being a couple of months away, it gave us plenty of time to gather materials. Begging, stealing and borrowing, we had a massive heap of stuff, and when the time came, made a bommie in Phil's back ally. The great night arrived and it went up like the towering inferno. It was obviously too big, because it burned next door's gate to a black mess and the fall-out from chucking cardboard boxes on from Phil's dad's flour store landed in everybody's back yard. Some complained about some washing being ruined to Phil's dad – well, fancy hanging washing out on November 5th! Still, it wasn't my fault!

Phil's dad and mum weren't badly off for money having a shop, so Phil nearly always got what he wanted. He had some good fishing tackle, a racing bike and a small drum kit which he had in his bedroom. I would pester to have a go on it. His mum didn't mind as long as I kept the noise down. Phil also had a guitar, just an acoustic one, a bit out of tune, but it made a noise. I would bash out a racket while Phil twanged away. It sounded crap, but we enjoyed it. Having a go on Phil's kit made me want a set of my own. Again, pester, pester, pester to Mum and Grandma. The answer was always the same, 'No.' But I was determined to wear them down to my request. I said I would get a paper round to help pay for it. I got on their nerves. Through a friend, I got to know of a kit that was being sold second-hand for £50. A hell of a lot of money, but I was determined. I went to have a look at it. On High Walton Road, a lad was selling his kit. He was in a band called "The Alpines". It was a Premier set, a bit bashed up. I had a go on it, but just made a noise. He showed me what he could do, it sounded fab. I had to have it. So back home, I said if I could buy it, I would find somewhere to practise as they wouldn't have it in the house because all the neighbours would complain. I was getting closer. If they were to help me buy it, I said don't get me anything for Christmas or birthdays for years. Very, very reluctantly, they said maybe. I was getting even closer. I tried everywhere to store my drum kit – the church hall, an empty shed in the vicarage grounds, even a storeroom above the local corner shop. No one would take me on. Then a chance, Phil's gran had a house near the river with an empty garage. She said I could use it, but wouldn't take any responsibility for it. This looked promising. To prove my worth, I took a paper round and also was prepared to do a morning milk round as well before school.

'Oh well, go on then,' said Mum.

I couldn't get down to Higher Walton Road fast enough. When I did, I was told it had been sold. My world fell apart, so near as well. I kept looking in the adverts in the shop windows for another, but there was nothing. The wanting gradually waned from me, then I gave up. It wasn't to be.

While I was asking the vicar if I could use the church hall, Mum told me to ask him about confirmation classes and to enrol for the next session. I wasn't bothered about the classes, in fact, religion didn't interest me at all, but I had to agree to Mum's request just to keep her on my side. I was twelve or thirteen at the time when I went to my first lesson at St Mary's church. I remember it well. It was dark and chucking it down. On entering St Mary's Street, it started to thunder. The silhouette of the church just looked like something out of a horror movie, being backlit from the lightning. Who was I going to meet here, the vicar or Dracula. The church doors were open, I entered, the church was in darkness apart from a tiny light at the far end coming from the vestry. I shouted, 'Hello, I'm here.' The door at the other end slowly opened and the dark figure said, 'Come in.' I think it was Dracula. Walking down the knave hearing my own footsteps, I felt like I was approaching my doom. Imagining skeletal hands reaching out from the empty dark pews making a grab for me. I couldn't get into the vestry fast enough. There were 4 other kids in there. I knew a couple of them from school. We were given a prayer book and some writing paper and pencils. I was bored already. We started off with a prayer and then we had to open a bible and start to copy some stuff I didn't understand. Then the vicar started to spout off about this and that. Why do I have to be told what to believe? I'm more practical than spiritual. Was this the start of a gentle brainwashing? My bible has always been a fishing tackle catalogue and my church, the river. I didn't want this fella telling me all about right or wrong, I knew that. I've nothing against people absorbing this stuff and practising their religion, but don't try and throw it down someone else's neck who has their own beliefs.

My inner self was and always will be, enjoy life, do no harm to anyone nor anything (except catching fish) and have fun. Life is really short. You're born and you die and you fill the middle bit in the best you can. I want to use my time by appreciating the natural world, not the spiritual one. I believe that when we snuff it, that's it, we don't go to the cover of a Jehovah witness booklet where the sky is always blue, the odd wild animal walks serenely by and people of all colours pick fruit and smell wild flowers. If we aren't cremated, we end up a smelly, mushy mess. Not a pleasant thought, but that's the reality. We don't go to some figment of someone's imagination, or to a place that is documented in a book. Anyway, I had to go along with the confirmation lessons and I was confirmed in February 1961 in St Matthew's church, Preston, by the Bishop of Blackburn. We had to go up to him 2 at a time to be blessed. He would put a hand on each head and say a few words. I was the last up, so I had 2 hands on my head. Mum said I was lucky, I got a double do. She couldn't wait to take me for my first communion at St Mary's after that. Now skilled in the art of looking solemn and attentive. Going up to the altar rail for a sip of wine and a bit of bread didn't mean anything to me, although I knew what it signified. Even having to go to Sunday evening service was a total bore. I would mime to the hymns and sit with one eye open during prayers, not taking any notice, thinking I could be in the open air enjoying real life. I went along with it for a while, and then started to protest only to be told it was doing me good. It wasn't. Gradually, it tailed off, but Mum continued to go.

CHAPTER 5
MEETING DAD AND BULLIES

One Sunday morning, when Mum was at church and Grandma was across the street talking to a neighbour, I had a little rummage in a few drawers in the bedrooms. I knew what was in mine, but Mum's drawers and Grandma's were forbidden territory. Still, I had a peep and uncovered a wedding album of Mum's wedding, but found something that puzzled me. All the photos of my dad had his face cut out of the pictures. I reasoned this must have been done to take him out of our lives and it puzzled me greatly. I put things back and covered my tracks, but couldn't get it from my mind. I never really, until then, worried about not having a dad around like all the other kids in the street. I had to satisfy my curiosity, but how? I took my opportunity when Grandma went out to play at a local whist drive and asked Mum why have I not got a dad. She initially looked shocked at my question, then said, 'I suppose your old enough now to be told.' This was the first time in my life that Dad's name was ever mentioned. I listened carefully.

She told me his name was William Henry Rampling and they married at St Mary's church in 1947. I gathered that Granddad and Grandma didn't approve of him and things didn't work out between them. She didn't go into any more detail and still, even today, I don't know the real reason. I asked if she had any pictures of him, she said no, he's gone, finished, that's enough. It wasn't until many years later, when my two children were about the same age as me when I first enquired. Paul, my son, asked me who his real granddad was. I was dumbstruck, a question that came out of the blue and I couldn't give him a proper answer. I must find out this time. I firstly asked Mum if she didn't mind if I tried to find him. By this time, Grandma had passed away and Mum had mellowed a bit. She said go ahead. Well, it didn't take much investigating. I simply looked in the phone book and there he was – RAMPLING, WILLIAM HENRY, Woodville Road, Penwortham, Preston. I didn't have the nerve to ring him, so decided to write him a letter. I explained who I was and the reason for writing. I tore up a page or two and rewrote it a few times, struggling to find the right words. The letter ended by saying, 'If you decided not to respond for your own reasons, I quite understand and I am sorry to have troubled you, but I wish you well.' Hovering at the mouth of the post box, do I or not. In it went/ I heard nothing for about a week or so and thought that was the end of the matter. Then, one evening, the phone rang. I picked it up, 'Hello.'

'Alan?'

'Yes.'

'It's your dad.'

All I could say was a stupid, 'Oh.' He told me that he had received the letter and thanked me very much for it. He said that after he had read it, it brought a tear to his eye. Both of us had then an awkward silence. I didn't know how to respond except thinking to myself this is the first time in my life, I was in my 30s by then, that I had ever heard him. I just wanted him to keep talking, but he went quiet as well.

'Look,' he said. 'Let's meet up somewhere.' He said he couldn't wait to see me.

The feeling was mutual, neither could I. We arranged to meet at a local pub, The Plough Inn on Blackpool Road, its long since been demolished.

'How will I recognise you? I've never seen you before.' I asked.

'I'll be in my car, a red Volvo.'

'Okay, I'll be in my yellow Fiesta.'

I arrived at a set time to find his car near the entrance. He got out as I entered. After parking up, I got out and we walked towards each other. He held out his hand, we shook hands then put arms around each other and embraced. I was shaking like a leaf and so was he.

'Come on, let's have a drink,' he said. 'This is such a wonderful day,' and thanked me for taking the initiative of the letter. He told me he had it in his wallet and it would be with him wherever he went.

After a short period of awkwardness, we relaxed in each other's company. Telling me he would have never contacted me because many years ago when he left Mercer Street, he had been living with Granddad and Grandma as well, Granddad said never to contact the boy again, he had agreed. He didn't go into too much detail of why my mum and he split and divorced and now it didn't really matter. I didn't quiz any further on that. He said, 'Do you realise I had a half-sister?' I hadn't a clue. To say it took me by surprise is an understatement.

Her name is Angela Jane Rampling, she was born after he remarried his second wife, Jean. I immediately realised that her initials where the same as mine – AJR. I asked if this was a coincidence. 'No,' he said. 'I wanted something of you to be reflected in her and so the name was chosen.'

He told Angela that he was going to meet me and that she wanted to meet me too.

'Do you know anything of your ancestry?' he asked.

'Only from my mum's side,' I replied.

'Well, you come from an aristocracy background you know.'

'Bloody hell! I must be in line to the throne, then. Probably about 10000th,' I joked. He laughed.

We were beginning to relax more with each other by then and enjoying each other's company. Apparently, my great, great grandfather was a family member of the Early of Derby. One of the maids produced a little girl after a fling with him and she was kept in service at Knowsley Hall to protect shame being thrown upon the Derby family. That little girl became my great, great grandmother on Dad's side. When he himself found this out may years earlier, he investigated it with the help of a solicitor and found it was indeed true. The findings were in writing in the archives of a solicitor's office somewhere in Liverpool. This meeting with Dad was becoming mind-blowing. He said all these years he had never forgotten me and he had quietly supported me financially. On one occasion, he had spotted Mum and me in town on our usual shopping spree. He wanted to stop and introduce himself to me, but thought otherwise keeping true to his promise to Granddad. He said it was a very happy and at the same time a very sad day when he saw us. He apparently followed us around town for an hour or two unknown to us, thinking what a fine boy I looked. But I was so near and yet so far from him. Our meeting finished just short of closing time. We had been chatting for two and a half hours.

On leaving, he invited me to his house to meet his wife and he would arrange for Angela to be there as well. It was fixed for a week's time. I went armed with a few family photos and a pot plant gift for Jean. On entering, I was met by Bill and Jean and hugged. Jean said Angela was upstairs and that she would go and get her. Angela came down and we just stood looking at each other for what seemed ages. We were introduced and started chatting while Jean put the kettle on. She put on a bit of a fuss, best china cups and a plate of sandwiches and Dundee cake came out. I felt right at home, they made me feel very welcome. Angela and I arranged to go out for a meal soon. I would bring along Pauline, my wife, and she'd bring Dave, her partner. She said when she found out about me, when she was very young, she wanted to meet me and missed having a brother. It would have been fun, doing all the things that the years took from us. We kept in touch with letters and occasions cards for a long time. It was hard to meet regularly as she worked as a nurse doing shifts in hospital.

A few short years later, Bill died. I went to his funeral at Preston crematorium. I just sat at the back quietly. The place was packed, not only with family, but army personnel as well. The British Legion formed a guard of honour. After the service, I quietly made my way out, but was stopped by a stranger. He said, 'Are you Alan?'

'Yes,' I said.

'Bill's told me all about you and how proud he was of you.' He shook my hand and left to point me out to the others who turned around. At this stage, I felt a bit awkward so hot-footed it back to the car. I was invited to Jean's house on numerous occasions and she told me more about Dad. He was a very well-respected member of the forces and that at the end of the war, during the liberation of the concentration camps, he was the third British soldier through the gates of Belsen. He stayed in the camp trying to save as many as he could, unfortunately he contracted typhus while there and was sent to hospital to recover. For his efforts, and indeed he did save a number of lives, he was awarded a medal and oak leaf. This was presented to me by Angela years later along with all his other medals. They are all tucked away. I will treasure them always. They will be handed on to my son in time, as a remembrance and contact with his granddad he never knew. Jean passed away a couple of years ago, but Angela and I keep in contact sometimes. Anyway, back to equally important stuff.

One subject at school that I really took to was science. Considering I wasn't doing too badly at it, the science master, Mr Addison or "Daddy Addy" as he was nicknamed, promoted Eddie Taylor and me to science monitors. A choice job. Just before double science after lunchtime, we were allowed into the lab to prepare things for the lesson. Daddy Addy would give us our instructions during morning break, writing things like "twelve Bunsen burners on benches", "twelve tripods", "six tubes per station", "clean board", etc. The laboratory was unlocked and we had the free run of the place until lesson started. I didn't mind being a monitor as it kept me away from the prowling misfits who roamed around picking fights. Eddie was a nutter who would do anything for a laugh. One day, we met in the lab to get things ready. He was very excited as his kid brother had told him how to make a massive stink bomb. Well, after apparatus was positioned, we entered the store room, it was never locked. There were powders, chemicals and mixtures of all sorts. Rows of big bottles in easy reach, all ready for us to experiment with. So, armed with Eddie's scant knowledge, we began to make the world's biggest stink bomb. Half a beaker of sulphur powder was mixed with half a beaker of iron fillings, then placed on a large gauze on top of a tripod and a Bunsen burner was lit under it. The flame, at full bore, reduced the mix to a charred lump, something resembling a large chunk of solid ash. Eddie said his kid brother said we needed to dunk this in a bowl of hydrochloric acid. There was loads of it on the store room shelf, so we poured some into a glass bowl and threw the lump into it. It started to bubble and fizz straight away and a most awful, sickening stink emitted from it. We tried to stop it by putting a board over it, but it kept on fizzing even more. Eddie opened the classroom door, any kids coming past were either almost throwing up or were mightily impressed. The pong became unbearable. Daddy Addy arrived to see what the commotion was about and the bollocking we got was worse than the stink. We were fired from being monitors forthwith and the lesson was cancelled. All the class, except us two, had double library, much to their horror. We ended up in the headmaster's room for a whack and 200 lines as well. All the kids wanted the recipe for the stink bomb and it went round school as well, but I don't think anyone achieved the dizzy heights of success that Eddie and me managed. The lab was locked after that and no one was allowed in before lessons. I think Daddy Addy had a bollocking as well.

It didn't stop us experimenting though. Another bright idea was to make a mini-bomb. It took a lot of planning. Eddie, Phil, Dave, Dave and me met at Phil's house prior to bonfire night when the shops were full of fireworks. He reckoned if we obtained enough 1d bangers, open them up and pour all the explosive powder into a bigger container, we could blow something up. It sounded good to me. So, using our spends wisely, we collected loads of 1d bangers. The container was a toiler roll holder sealed at the bottom with paper and sticky tape. Sealed the same way at the top, a 2d banger, called an "Atom bomb", was stuck into it. This was the detonator. We were like mad scientists. We even decorated the toilet roll with big letters saying "BOMB". We couldn't wait for Guy Fawkes night. We were ready to release our beast. This next bit is a bit crass, but it's what we did. Phil thought it would be a laugh if the big banger had a dollop of horse shit stuck on it. It would create shit shrapnel as well. An excellent idea. The horse muck was easy to collect, there was always a few cobbles of it about in the street, although it was always cleaned up by anyone growing spuds in their back yards or nearby allotments. Phil got quite a bit in a bag and the great night approached. We all met at the local meeting place, "the Loney Hill". It was a rough track leading to the river away from the eyes of parents. The dollop was duly placed near the street lamp, it acted as a holder for the bog roll tube as well. I had the honour of lighting it. I did. We all stood well back and waited for Armageddon. The explosion was huge. In a split second, Preston was almost wiped off the map. The horse muck splattered all up the lamppost and beyond. What a way to enjoy yourself and lose what bit of money we had in less than a second. It was subject to much laughter for ages. We were quite proud of our genius. Looking back and recalling these pranks we got up to, is, in a way, self-satisfying and a bit, I say a bit, educational. How many kids today will look back as I have and think of dozens and dozens of capers involving inventive play. Many will only recall years of games on electronic devices that has been invented for them.

Mum once took me to a jumble sale at St Matthew's one night. I didn't want to go, but she didn't trust me on my own. I don't know why. Grandma had gone playing dominoes at the Friendship Club which would have meant leaving me at home. Anyway, off we went. While she was rummaging through heaps of clothes, I had a wander around and came across a book stall. All boring stuff except one that caught my eye. It was called *100 Things a Boy Can Make* and it cost 3d. I bought it with my own spends, I also got a *Vimto* book free with it as well. That contained loads of interesting facts. Mum thought I'd spent well, so did I. In the book, amongst other things, was instructions to make a working rocket out of everyday items. Items required were 2 cylindrical washing up liquid bottles, 4 canes, string, 1 football inflater valve, scissors and pencil. All items, except the 2 bottles, were duly collected. I borrowed a valve from my cousin who played a lot of footy. I had one, but the other was only just opened. I couldn't wait a week or two for it, I had to construct the rocket right away. I pestered and pestered, even squirting some down the sink to give it a helping hand. Mum got fed up, so she emptied it into a milk bottle and told me to clear off. Cutting the top 3 inches off one bottle, this was forced on the bottom of the other which made the nose cone. Two circles of the remaining bottle, about 1 inch wide, were cut off and slid onto the bottom of the rocket. These were to hold the fins that were fashioned from the cut tube. The launch pad was simply made by pushing 4 sticks into the ground and wrapping a piece of string around it 6 inches from the ground. This supported the rocket for launch. The squirty nozzle of the rocket was taken off and filled 1/3 full of water and then the nozzle replaced. The inflater valve was inserted into it and attached to a foot pump. The air pressure built up and forced the cap off, the water, under pressure, acted as a propellant. So armed with my Ramps Rocket Mk I, I called for Graham to help launch it. We decided the launch site would be at the lodge bank at the bottom of the street. Careful adjustments of the sticks supported the rocket in a vertical position and I pumped away. The pressure was enormous in the bottle as it began to bulge. A few more pumps forced

49

the cap off and "whoosh", up it went higher than the houses and came down in one piece. A second attempt for it to cross the lodge by placing the sticks at an angle was also successful, but a third attempt wasn't. The bottle split and we got showered with water, but what fun.

All the kids were starting to make them. Some decorating them, even attempted to build parachutes into them, but these were useless. We looked through everyone's bins and asked neighbours for any empty bottles. We were every mum's annoyance. If only mum knew what we got up to on our adventures, she would have had a duck fit.

Swimming one day in the River Brock near Garstang under a small waterfall was fun until I got caught in a swirling current. I swallowed loads of water and probably would have drowned if it hadn't been for Colin handing me a branch to pull me in. That really was very scary and the nearest I've ever been to croaking it. I remember, just before he pulled me in after panicking and swallowing water, I felt a calm come over me, a sort of feeling that this is the end.

The first year of secondary school, I didn't do too badly, starting off in the "A" stream until I got on the radar of the bullies. Most of them were in the "D" stream. Always in a gang, they would filter out any sensitive soul. One latched onto me, a lad called Alan. He had a bigger brother in a higher year and would go around with him looking for trouble. When he kept asking me for a fight, I would always refuse, frightened of getting glasses broken and knowing Mum didn't have much money to get them fixed. Colin said to me, 'Have him a scrap. Go on, do him.' So, one break time, Alan caught me in the bogs and said, 'I'm going to smash your face in.' Something came over me and I said, Not if I smashed yours in first.' He went sort of quiet. I asked him if he still wanted a fight to settle it. 'Yes,' he said, so I suggested it took place at the top of Loney Hill near where we both lived.

'But,' I said. 'Just you and me. No one else. Don't bring big bro, mates or anyone, and neither will I.' Six o'clock was agreed for that night

Going home that night I was shaking like a leaf. I couldn't eat my tea and resigned myself to death. Still, I couldn't back out now. At 6pm, I waited at the lamppost at Loney Hill. I hung around for about an hour, but he didn't show, so I went home. If he had have shown up, I'm convinced I would have killed the little squirt, although I would have endured a battering as well. Next day, I confronted him, 'Where were you?'

'Couldn't come. Something on,' he said and went away.

For some reason, he never bothered me again.

Bullying was rife in Fishwick School with the teachers turning a blind eye most of the time. I was approached again that year by another gang. They really put the frighteners on me, threatening to break my glasses and telling me that if I passed my exams, they would kill me. I couldn't handle it this time and it got worse. All this really got to me, but I kept it to myself. I was in a constant state of worry. Scared of going to school, scared of playing out, I became a nervous wreck, so much so, that I failed my exams. In fact, I came bottom of the class. When Mr Steele, the deputy head, read out the positions, everyone laughed. I felt really bad. So I was dropped into the "B" stream the next year. The bullying continued, even my friend, David, got it as well, but he told his dad. One morning, David's dad arrived at school just before take in and the bully was pointed out to him. He got hold of him and slammed him up against the wall and read him the riot act. Things went quiet for a while, but started again with just me in the firing line. I endured more of it. It was because of this, I didn't reach my full potential at school. When he left at Christmas, the feeling of a weight being lifted was wonderful. I began really to fly at lessons, my confidence soared and I achieved excellent results on leaving the following summer. The guy in question lives not too far from me now. I still recognise him. For what he put me through all those years ago, I could never forgive him. I know I could have done better at school and gone on to further education, but such was his influence, I hid myself most of the time.

Getting a job in those days was really easy. Everywhere there were advertisements for apprentices for school leavers, whether you had qualifications or not. I was told by the "School to Work" employment officers that anyone with qualifications should go into office work and banking, anyone who didn't have qualifications got a labourer's job doing manual work. I just couldn't wait to leave school. I had a belly full of it. My form master, Mr Steele, tried to persuade me to go for ULCI or GCE exams. I wasn't interested, so I applied for a job as a young garden labourer at Preston Corporation Parks Dept.

CHAPTER 6
FIRST STEPS

It looked like something out of Charles Dickens 'Christmas Carol', when I first entered the park office at Miller Park, Preston in mid-July, 1963 looking for a job as a gardener. My Aunty Mary took me because she knew where it was. My mother would have come as well, but she was working at the time and couldn't get the time off. My Uncle Jack (Mum and Mary's brother) had been employed by Preston Corporation for some years and suggested it might be a good job to go for.

There was, I recall, a huge old writing desk in one corner of the office that was heavily ink stained, especially around a thick glass ink well and pen stand. On the top stood an old photograph of a couple sitting on a bench and a huge dog sat with them. The photo had a crease down the middle suggesting it had been roughly stored before being rescued and displayed. I never found out who they were.

On top of the desk was, of all things, a metronome, a couple of old brass candlesticks without candles and a couple of gardening books on top of which was a heavy glass ashtray with the remnants of a couple of cigar butts.

The floor was green linoleum with a rug in the middle, it had a few burn holes in it, probably it once sat up against the tile fireplace and obtained it's injuries when coal fell from the grate.

Everything seemed a light brown colour, the result, no doubt, of the park superintendent, Mr Pearson, and his deputy, Mr Cross, smoking cigars and Senior Service full strength in there all day.

Mr Pearson, or AV as some called him because his first names were Arnold Victor, was well respected by everyone. An absolute fountain of horticultural knowledge gained not only from his father, who was, I believe, a head gardener at some stately home, but a very experienced landsman in his own right.

He lived in a park "grace and favour" home at the gates to Avenham Park with is wife and daughter, Susan, who was quite attractive. She always got a few looks from the greenhouse lads when she shimmied past. She was gorgeous and knew it, completely out of our league.

Mr Cross, 'Walter' to the head boys, but always Mr Cross to the lads, also lived in a park house in nearby Miller Park: a most attractive place with a wonderful view of the valley and river Ribble in the distance. He also had a daughter by the name of Linda. A tall girl, a bit snobby, good looking, but again out of our league. And so I was shown to a chair between two filing cabinets for my interview.

'Name?'

'Alan Rampling.'

'Why do you want to be a gardener?'

'Because my Uncle John is a gardener, he is in charge of the bowling greens and said it's a good job to be in, so here I am.'

'When can you start?'

'Any time, I leave school next Friday.'

'OK, start Monday, is that right for you?'

'Yes.'

That was the interview

At this stage, Mr Cross disappeared into another room and returned with a chap called Bill Viner, he was Parks Secretary, holding a booklet.

Bill said, '£4.1.2d a week for 45 hours. 7.30am start, 5.30pm finish, OK?'

'Yes, sir.'

'Right then, report to the greenhouses to Harry Billington, bring a pack lunch, a drink and don't be late. We will give you a 6 month trial and a review after that.'

I felt very small waiting at the bus stop on my first morning standing amongst flat caps and haversacks. I really did feel like a "first day at worker". A 3½d trip, it stopped in town, followed by a fifteen minute walk to work. As I approached the greenhouses, a noisy Norton motorbike passed me, obviously going to the same place: a fellow worker on his way in. By the time I reached the potting shed/ mess room, the guy on the bike was already there.

'I have to report to Harry,' I said. 'I'm new.'

'I'm Peter,' he said, 'and Harry doesn't come in before 9am. He goes via the Town Hall to pick up the mail and waters the plants there first.'

With that, I wandered into the shed and what a strange world it looked and smelled. The mess room didn't defy the Trades Description Act either: it was a mess! In the room was an old drop-leaf table full of cup rings, a dart board, a collection of odd chairs and books, and old Belfast sink set on a heap of bricks and one cold tap, an electric cooker with an assortment of pans and kettles on it. The resident cat just looked me up and down in disgust and left. So I sat down on a chair to wait for Harry.

'Can't sit there,' said Peter, 'that's Harry's. You sit on that low cupboard under the window."

I did as I was told, by this time feeling very nervous not knowing what was expected of me.

'What's your name?' Peter asked.

'Alan.'

It was then 2 more lads came in, Dave and Bill, and an old guy called Ray Bowman. He looked a bit like Oliver Hardy and was nice to talk to. Then came "ol' one leg" as Peter called him. A chap on crutches with one leg, his other trouser leg was folded up and tucked into his belt. Ken was an ex-Canadian football player who lost his leg after a tragic accident, I don't know how, somehow I daren't ask. I felt sorry for him at first, but he very soon became a pain in the arse: "bring me this", "carry me that", he treated me like his personal slave, which I suppose I was, being known as a young gardener/labourer, and commonly called "Nipper" by the lads.

And so my working life began on 31st July, 1963, the second week of the Preston holidays, by being taken onto the adjacent park to help out on the annual horse show.

It was a beautiful hot, sunny day and my first job was to help put up all the fold-up chairs out on the park valley. There seemed to be hundreds of the things to stand up. The other lads put up the horse jumps. Later, I was consigned to the corral jump, putting the poles back up if they were knocked down. Squatting down next to it was a scary sight, watching the powerful horses coming full belt a few feet away (no such thing as health and safety then) as the ground shook, but all exciting stuff.

After my butties at dinner time, I was introduced to a bit of alcohol by Peter.

Time for a rhyme perhaps:

1953 at Miller Park fountain, Preston.
Years later was head gardener.

Age 11. Another bad haircut.

1960s. Billy, Arthur, Bob and me (dig the hair, man!)

Referring to the steps, not me.

That's me in the middle.

Brian, Nick Parks and me in front of our council float, 2012.

First gold medal,
Tatton Park Flower Show.

Another gold, Southport Flower Show.

Gold medal, 2014. Tatton Park Flower Show.

The Team receiving a gold medal from Mayor of Preston, 2014.
Shaun, Brian, Mayor, me, Don and Trev.

Miller Park, Preston, on a beautiful
summer's day.

64 years on from the cover picture.

HORSE SHOW DAY

It was in July of '63
When Adam was a Lad
I went for a job on Preston Parks
With my Aunty Mary, I had no dad.

He starts work on Monday
Said Mr Pearson, a job no more to seek
Seven-thirty start and finish half five
For £4.1.2d a week

Started work on horse show day
I couldn't believe my luck
My first job on Avenham Park
Putting jumps back up

Nice and sunny, this was really good
And lots of drinks we did sup
But job two didn't suit, I remember it now
Cleaning horse muck up

'Come on Alan, I'll buy you a drink,'
Said Peter, a pint of shandy.
Never tried it before,
It made my legs go bandy.

During the afternoon, I had another
Me and Peter in a big marquee
I got onto mild, then onto bitter.
Felt sick and wanted to pee.

I excused myself, I had to go
A funny feeling inside my tum.
In a cold sweat, head down bog,
Oh dear, up it come.

I've never forgotten that very first day.
New mates, good job, good crack.
All gone now, never to return,
Still, it's good to look back.

The day finished with me being told to go to the eatery tent to pick up the judges teas. At the marquee, I was told to go behind a screen and the food would be issued to me. Apart from the food, it was full of flies as well as a small dog sniffing around the sandwiches stacked in plastic crates on the ground.

The following days seemed very long indeed and I had all kinds of crap jobs put on me from cleaning clay pots and toilet cleaning (I seem to smell permanently of Jeyes Fluid). The bog in question was basically a large bucket with a wooden toilet seat plonked on it, in a shed. My job every day was to empty it before going home by digging a deep hole behind the greenhouses, pour in the contents and fill it in. Harry always insisted that a hole at least a spade depth, but after a few days of this, I got a bit pissed off so I just dug a shallow scrape, poured in the doings with my jumper pulled up over my nose and mouth then topped it with an inch or 2 of soil, patting it with the back of the spade which made it wobble.

One morning, Mr Pearson went behind the greenhouse with Harry looking to have the ventilators repaired. On arriving back at the potting shed, Harry gave me a dirty look that made me think, 'Oh shit.' Yes, Mr Pearson had stepped right into last night's offerings covering his brogues with crap. Not only was Harry mad, Mr Pearson was as well and so my first bollocking took place.

From then on, all shit holes were of contract depth. I was also schooled in a very important nippering matter: looking after the foreman's every need. Fetch me, bring me, carry me and also going for chips and making his tea. On instruction, I was to look into his haversack to see if he had a pie, casserole or soup to put in the oven for his dinner. On one occasion, I remember he had some home-made soup. This is what happened:

HARRY'S PEA SOUP

Now, one of my jobs as a nipper
Was to ask the foreman to see
If he had some soup to put on for his dinner
Usually mushroom, tomato or pea.

One day he said he had some pea soup
Homemade by his wife's fair hand.
'Just warm it up for 12 minutes,
And for five, let it stand.'

So I put it on at quarter to twelve,
Not to late or too soon,
So Harry could sit and enjoy his soup
On the very dot of noon.

'Ee, that smells good,' said Harry
As he washed his hands of dirt.
Then he sat down and dunked some bread
And with a spoon began to slurp.

Suddenly, things turned nasty
As a pea got stuck in his throat.
He turned bright red and then quite blue
Poor Henry had begun to choke.

'Smack him ont' back,' said Peter.
To remove the offending pea.
'I'm not doing it,' said Raymond.
'Let the bugger dee.'

So Peter shot up from his seat
And with such a heavy clout
Wacked Harry ont' back, Harry coughed
And the offending pea shot out.

Now Harry had heard what Raymond had said
And from then on his presence did poop.
They never spoke for many a while
All because of Harry's pea soup.

One of the things that I envied was watching the other guys going out in the wagon doing floral decoration jobs. We used to have regular work: putting fresh plants and flowers in the town hall foyer and changing on a regular basis the flowers in the meeting rooms and lunch room in the municipal building. All the lads were hoping to be in Harry's favour for doing this, because when the foreman got there, he would be kept talking for ages by the porters and the mayor's attendant, so the lads would disappear into the kitchens and brew up. So, whoever was chosen to give Harry a hand was sure to have a scive.

Going out in the wagon with either Jim or Harold in the early days was always an occasion of excitement. My turn came one day when I was chosen to go with him in the 'tipper' to do an important job. It was, in fact, my very first outing and boy, was I worked up about it as Jim came to pick me at 1 o'clock. We were to go to Moor Park, which was about a twenty minute trip, to pick up some plants from Billy Smart's circus which had been performing in the town for the last week. The plants had been at the main entrance of the big top and booking office, and while we were there, we had to find Howard to pick up payment. Plants were duly collected – a few conifers and shrubs, that's all – and we began looking for Howard. After a few enquiries, we found him. He led us round the back of a load of caravans, then between the menagerie where some docile-looking big cats where taking a bit of interest in what we were doing. The payment turned out to be an enormous, steaming heap of animal shit all mixed up with straw and cage sweepings.

'Take what you want,' he said and then disappeared.

Jim backed his lorry through the gates and forked most of it on. On returning to the office at Miller, we were told to drop it at the bottom of the boss's plot. The veg he grew on there was always top quality, no doubt the result of last year's payment. Talking about the plot, it was my job to keep it weed free, my only horticultural job at present apart from cleaning thousands of clay pots.

One Friday, I was given a very important job: to get a collection of vegetables for the boss's wife for the weekend. I hope this explains what happened, I've called it:

COS CUTTING

Now as a nipper of only 15
Amongst the jobs that I got
Was to take a hoe and once a week
Weed the boss's plot.

Then on the last Friday of my very first month
I got an order from the boss
To gather some spuds and beans for weekend
Some onions and some cos.

Well how many? I don't know.
I suppose I ought to ask
But I daren't, so got a barrow
And just got on wit' task.

A bucket o' spuds and the same of beans
But how many lettuce shall I pull?
At a guess, I'd say six or seven.
At that, my barrow was full.

On't way back to Boss's house
He shouted from window, 'Oi, son.
'Just leave 'em on't doorstop, and as for lettuce
'I only want one.'

It's a good job he didn't see inside barrow
'Cause I'd covered it with a sack.
I thought, 'Oops, I cut too many,'
So I decided to put some back.

I plonked them down on top of the soil
Hoping no one would tell.
But within a couple of hours int sunshine
They weren't looking all that well.

On the Monday morning, he went as usual
To check on spuds and peas.
Seeing his lettuce all wilted like,
Said, 'Ee, Alan. Somats 'ad these.'

Well, I looked puzzled best I could.
'Pull 'em up and chuck em away.'
It were only me who knew how they died.
Well, it was … until today.

Around about that time, I felt I was becoming "one of the lads"
and it was clear I was being accepted when they invited me to be
in goal the next time 'Harry went out'. And so it was, a regular
occurrence that he went out solo every other Monday to change
flowers in the registrar office. I think he went to chat up one of the
registrars who he thought was fit. Well, he was in his late 50s and
she must have been 60. We could tell something was going on,
because he always put his 'going home' cap on. Anyway, this is
what happened that day.

MICE WILL PLAY

Now Harry was the foreman
At the greenhouses where I did work.
He'd stand no messing, or fooling about
And no jobs were you to shirk.

One day, he went out int' wagon
To do a flower dec job,
So the lads he left had a kick about.
Me, Peter and Bob.

I were int' goal (a greenhouse door)
And Bob came in from the right
On to Peter's head a shot at goal.
Then, we all went sickly white.

The ball had gone through greenhouse window
With a terrible almighty crash,
Rolled ont' bench then ont' floor
Leaving smashed plants and glass.

Well, I got blame for not saving it.
Pete said, 'We'll all get the sack.'
We just stood there shaking in fear
Because Harry would soon be back.

This called for a fast solution.
We had to act as quick as a flash.
I got some putty, Bob cleaned up
And Peter got some new glass.

The job was done in 10 minutes flat
Five more and Harry arrived.
If only he knew the mice had played.
We never would have survived.

By now I was getting used to the run of the place. I had my daily duties to attend to. Cleaning the office every morning, I was schooled by Harry to dust all the desks and vacuum the carpet (that I was finally glad to see the back of). The vacuum must have been a hundred years old, it was the size of a tank sounded like one. It finally blew up one morning and I thought, 'Hurrah, a new one,' but no, I had to go up to the superintendent's house and borrow Mrs Pearson's, use it, then take it back.

After cleaning the office (I cut a few corners, I can tell you) the final chore was to empty the waste paper baskets and burn the contents. Harry insisted that every piece of paper was to be burned, as there were some very sensitive information in there. What sensitive information? I didn't find any. I used to read everything and never found any nuclear secrets.

One morning, I was caught red-handed. Harry arrived earlier than usual and bobbed into the office to check I was working. He caught me sat in Pearson's leather swivel chair, feet up on the desk reading all the mail in the bins. He was horrified and another bollocking took place. My jobs for the rest of the day was glass cleaning. Standing on a rickety set of steps wetting the glass with a hosepipe, scattering a light dusting of sand on, then scrubbing with an old-fashioned scrubbing brush nailed onto a ten foot wooden stick, then wash it off again. Punishment was complete, I thought, until the brush was taken from the stick and I was introduced to an enormous stock of clay pots. They had to be scrubbed then stacked in pyramids to dry.

He seemed from that day on to take a degree of dislike to me, always finding fault in whatever I was doing. After stomaching this for a month or two, I was getting pretty pissed off and was seriously considering a change of job. I was doing nothing but crap jobs and wasn't even being given the chance to do any sort of greenhouse work.

Every year, the nursery used to hold a Chrysanthemum show in November. After growing about 600 pots of Chrysanths, they were all brought into a greenhouse which had to be emptied first and scrubbed top to bottom by you know who. The show lasted 2 weeks and was open to the public. My orders were issued 1 week prior to the show, which very nearly decided enough was enough. It was Ray who took me to one side and told me to prepare myself for a job I probably wouldn't like (another one), but I had to do it as part of my young garden labourer duties. I was to leave the greenhouses after morning brew time in a few days' time with a set of sandwich boards advertising the Chrysanthemum show. I was to walk into the town centre via the park and wander around the busy high streets shouting 'Chrysanthemum show … daily … Miller Park' and show off the boards and direct the way to anyone who wanted to know. Bloody hell! This really worried me for days. The embarrassment of maybe seeing any of my old school mates, indeed anyone who knew me, would be the last straw. I had some pride after all.

I asked to see the boards that I had to wear, but was told they were being repainted at the Corporation painting depot and they would be delivered on the morning of my first day advertising in town in a few days' time. In those days, you didn't argue with any superiors. I had to do it, no question. The worry over this was tremendous. I couldn't sleep. Something had to be done, so without telling anyone (not even my mother) I decided to look for another job. In fact, anything would be better than the embarrassment I would have to endure. So, I went cold-calling for a job at the British Aerospace sports ground just over the road from where we were, but they didn't want anyone. So then, I was onto a carpet firm, Gainsborough Carpets, fitting firm just off the town centre. I was told there would be a chance of apprentice carpet fitter. The manager was on holiday, but was to return mid-week. This seemed like my hope of a job change. My first day of advertising was to be the following Monday and I was told to return for an interview at the carpet shop on Wednesday, so I would only have to endure a couple of days of wandering the streets with this stupid board on.

The day had arrived and I resigned myself to my fate. This is going to be bad! I was to put on Harry's flat cap as I was to look "earthy" and fitting for the job. Well, I looked a right pillock. The boards were on the way down from the paint shop and then I was coached in public speaking. 'Chrysanthemum show … daily … Miller Park.' I didn't have any baggin (brew) that morning and I felt like I was about to be executed. I felt sick.

After brew, I was given a last brush-up and told to wait at the office door for the boards to arrive. I waited and waited. People came and went from the office giving me funny looks as I was lurking about in Harry's flat cap. It was then Mr Pearson came out asking what the hell I was supposed to be doing. I told him why and he smile and said, 'You silly bugger, they are pulling your leg. There's no such thing.' Turning around, I could see all the lads, as well as Harry and Ray, pissing themselves laughing. That incident, I thought, brought me even closer to the staff, as it had been an old custom and all of them, at one stage or another, have done it. The feeling that I had been the brunt of a joke was nothing compared with the huge relief it was that I wouldn't have to do it.

I never did attend the interview at the carpet shop. Having the chance of going out in the wagon to do a floral decorating job was always a good crack to go on, it made the day go faster and it also gave the opportunity to see different people and places.

We were asked one day to decorate the stage front at the local Masonic Hall for the chairman's ball. Harry said I could help him with this as it would give me some experience. All he really wanted was for me to do all the lifting and shifting and sweep up really, but I couldn't wait to go. Harry had done this for years on an annual basis, but it wasn't his favourite venue. This is what happened that day:

TOO MANY CHIEFS

Henry once took me decorating,
A big job at the Masonic Hall.
It looked real good when we had finished,
Ready for the chairman's ball.

But Henry didn't like working there.
'Too many chiefs,' he'd say.
I didn't know what he meant,
But I did by the time we came away.

Don't like that there,
Change this and that.
Bring them plants over here.
We tried our best, then Henry stood still
And said, 'Now, look here.

'That's what thas ordered, that's what thas getten.'
I was right pleased with that.
They were all dumb struck as we made our way out.
'Alan, get me hat.'

'Too many chiefs,' he said under his breath.
'Come on, Alan, I've had me fill.
'George said it reet and that's all that matters.'
'Who's that?' I said, then Henry replied,
'It's 'im paying the bill.'

One day I remember about that time was a chap called Vinny. He worked in the local park as a labourer. He seemed a bit thick, but tall and very strong, a bit like Jethro Clampett from the TV show, *The Beverley Hillbillies*. Anyway, all the park ironwork (railings, gates, summerhouse and benches) were being painted and about 6 or 7 of the council's painters swelled the ranks of gardeners. The mess room was almost full to overcrowded. It was Vinny who was acting nipper at the time, so was expected to go out and get all the dinners from the various shops in the vicinity.

On this occasion, he had a shopping order: fish, chips, pies, fags, all sorts, so decided to fasten a cardboard box with string to his bicycle handlebars to contain the dinners. The pies went on the bottom of the box, followed by the fish and chips and a couple of newspapers on top for insulation. Peddling like crazy back to the park, the bottom of the cardboard box collapsed, resulting in 7 or 8 pies and a wrap or two of chips ending up in the front wheel getting well minced around the spokes. He arrived back almost in tears. Whoever didn't want dinner bringing back thought it was hilarious, those that got 'spoke pie' didn't think so. The conclusion to this was that one of the painters had a car, so he went out and bought everyone's dinner as well as treating Vinny to a free bag of chips. Happy days.

Vinny passed his motorbike test the week after, learning on a BSA Bantam. He couldn't learn on anything much bigger because 250cc was the maximum power you could learn on. He looked huge on that bike. After passing, he got a 750cc Royal Enfield Constellation, a beast of a thing, but at least it fit him better. One lunchtime, he asked me if I would like to go for a spin.

'But, I've no helmet or goggles or jacket.'

'Don't matter, just get on.'

Off we went like a bloody rocket out of the park. He didn't have any goggles on either, and as we were approaching the nearby bypass, he turned around, eyes streaming and said, 'Cling on.'

I already was as he let rip on the outside lane. I thought I was going to die. We got back to the park and I was a nervous wreck and freezing cold. His eyes were like 2 red marbles.

'Did you like that,' he said.

'No. I was frightened to death.'

That's the last time I went on that bike. Two days later, he smashed it up and broke his legs. He was off work for ages. That put me off speed forever. I prefer my breeches arse two stroke (a push bike).

CHAPTER 7
CHARACTERS AND COLLEGE

I don't know why, but land workers seem to spawn a degree of odd characters – well, it seems so to me. Each Friday afternoon was my major clean-up of our mess room: windows, table, cups and sink all had to be cleaned, floor swept and mopped. As it was almost weekend, I really didn't mind too much as all kinds of visitors used to come in the mess room. Most of the outside foremen would visit Harry during the afternoon to pay their coupon money. It was a syndicate for the pools, but it seemed to me like it was a couple of hour's skive for the foremen. They would all talk about the lazy buggers they had in their gangs, football, and all of them smoked like factory chimneys.

There was one in particular, he was the Avenham Park foreman at that time – I'll call him Mr Barker. He would arrive about 1.30pm on his little moped. When he got off it, it looked like he had just run here for he breathed really deeply and would cough his lungs up before saying, 'How do. Is it okay if I send the lad for some fags, Henry?'

"Aye, and while he's there, he can get me some as well."

So I asked Mr Barker what he wanted.

Putting 2 hands on the potting bench with a hunched back, he'd say, 'Get me a packet of … (cough, cough, cough) … Capstan … (cough) … Full Strength … (cough, cough, cough).' This was always followed by a long wheeze.

Harry always had Woodbines.

On returning, all the foremen would be there in a haze of smoke waiting then for Mrs Lee. She came from the town hall by taxi with the pay packets. All the names of staff were duly read out and crossed off a list. Then they would wander away with a pocket full of pay packets to give out to the lads. Mr Barker was always last to leave after first having a brew in a cup he always brought with him in a box at the back of his moped. You could make a reasonable brew in that pint pot without putting any tea leaves in as there was such a thick coat of tannin on it.

He passed away the next year. Pete said he died from TT poisoning.

'Never heard of that before,' I said.

'Guts and lungs full of tar and tannin,' he said.

There seemed to be no end of these fellas all eager to tell you of the war. One in particular revelled in it. Get him talking and you could have a good hour skive at least. I met him for the first time through rabbits. During summer, we had several hundred dahlias in open cloche frames that the local rabbit population made a meal of on a few occasions. Something had to be done about this rodent pollution. So muggins me was sent on a special mission to the allotment man, a guy called Barry. He looked after the local allotment site, cutting hedges, keeping vacant plots tidy, that sort of thing.

I found him after touring the allotment paths on my bike, he was sat in his shed, well, it was the only one with smoke coming out of not only the chimney, but the open door as well. He was sitting in a dusty old armchair wearing a collarless shirt, bib and brace overalls and the obligatory flat cap, smoking an obvious roll-up which was about as thick as a matchstick. He had his feet up on a long log, one end of which was stuck in an iron fire grate and the other end sticking out of the shed door on a couple of axle stands. The shed decorations consisted of a couple of foxtails and a bayonet which was hung behind the door.

'What's ta want, lad,' he said.

'Harry's sent me to ask if you can get rid of rabbits. They have been playing havoc with our dahlias.'

He threw his tiny dog end into the fire, then started cutting a piece of chewing baccy with a penknife and started to chew it.

'Aye, tell him I'll be or in't morning.'

'What's that big knife hung up there for?' I asked.

'For stabbing rats in't cage traps,' he said.

Charming!

On return, I told Harry that he'd be there in the morning.

Well, morning came and Barry had obviously been there a while, because he was sitting in Harry's chair when I walked in. I was looking around as I had the illusion of a neat row of bunnies hung up from the rafters, but there wasn't a one.

'Thall 'ave no more trouble wi them rabbats for a bit,' he said.

So the lads and me had a walk down to the frames. It was a scene of devastation. He had seen off a rabbit or 2 that's for sure, but also a hundred or so minced dahlia plants. Using a shotgun, he'd splattered everything in sight. Barry was still there when Harry arrived and he weren't too pleased with the result.

'Right, be seein' ya', he said and with a neatly aimed projectile of baccy spit, he set off back to his plots.

'Bloody hell,' Harry said. 'He's done more damage than the bloody rabbits.'

All the lads and me thought it was hilarious.

When, during the winter months, there wasn't much to do on the plots, Barry would come to help out on the park. He was a very slow worker, in fact, everything about him was non-urgent. I used to like asking him the time. 'Just a minute,' he would say. The trench coat would be slowly unbuttoned, followed by the Harris Tweed sports coat revealing a waistcoat. In one of the breast pockets he would produce a tobacco flake round tin, taking the top off, he would take out a small cloth bag. In it was a pocket watch. Glasses went on and staring at the watch he would reveal the time, after which the whole thing would happen again in reverse.

This guy, to me, seemed to move at the speed of nature – totally stress free. I think the only thing that bothered him was that it had to go dark at night and come light in the morning. Nothing else seemed to matter. My hero!

A young lad turned up one morning at the greenhouses. I was engaged in making the fire in the office when he walked in.

'I have to report here and see Harry,' he said. 'I'm a new starter.'

'What's your name,' I said.

'John Bee,' he replied in a really soft voice.

Harry arrived just then and told him to stick with me and that I'd show him 'the ropes'. I had an underling. My God, I felt like a father figure. John was really small and built like a pipe cleaner – a real squirt. I thought, 'I'll show you the ropes, all right,' and began my tortuous regime right away. Not only was he scrawny, he didn't have an ounce of strength as he felt it difficult to lift a wheelbarrow without anything in it. Little Johnny was very willing, but not very tall and even the long yard brush was taller than him.

I took great delight in giving him some of my crap jobs like emptying the bog can. His first time at doing this, I had to dig the hole (he couldn't handle a spade) then he brought the can that was sloshing about, emptied it into the hole and then threw up in it and started crying. I told him not to be so soft, but I also felt there was something else as well. He told me there and then he had lost his mum and dad earlier in the year and was finding life difficult. He was living with his aunty and uncle and made me promise not to say anything to the others. After that, I became really sorry for him and helped him all I could. We became good mates for the short time he was with us. He left us after about 3 months for a job at English Electric as a labourer. On his last day, he bought me a small bar of chocolate as a thank you for being his friend. A great little lad, I wished him well.

For a short spell of eighteen months, I worked on the adjacent park looking after the Japanese rock garden. It hadn't been cared for for over a year since the last bloke left. So I spent every day in there trying to pull it together. It was a very big job and bloody cold in winter. I had to have my brew outside on the rock garden in winter. The foreman, Dick, wouldn't allow me back into the mess room until dinner time. It was while I was there, one thing I always used to look forward to was every day a group of schoolgirls (all teenagers) came past the rock garden from the nearby convent. There were some real stunners amongst them. All the lads used to conveniently find a job on their route.

The girls dressed for hockey passed at about 1.15pm going to the playing fields at the other side of the river. Once again, vanity by us saw chests out, stomachs in and looking dangerous. They didn't take a blind bit of notice of us. Just a load of jumped up snobs we all thought, but they had been told not to engage in any conversation with anyone, especially the park lads by orders of the chief nun. This I know because it was about fifty years later that I married Elizabeth (my second wife) who was one of those girls. I once asked her if she still had that little short, green skirt and yellow blouse.

'No! Why, what *are* you thinking?' she said with a smile.

'Oh, nothing!'

Around about this time, I was taking an interest in girls. There were several in the vicinity of the park who were regular acquaintances. Each day I went for the dinners, first to the pie shop and then on to the chippy. Mr and Mrs Forrest owned the chippy and their daughter used to help out. Her name was Beth, boy did I fancy her. Up until then, I was not very successful with girls, all because I thought that girls didn't like boys that wore glasses and I had a sort of inferiority complex. But regular visits to the chippy gave me an opportunity to be on first name terms with her. Sometimes, I'd take my specs off before going in the shop and tried to make myself look cool, tucking my t-shirt tightly into my belt and chewing a non-existent piece of gum. One day, she gave me a free bag of chips. I thought that's it, I've pulled. We're going to date, get married, have kids. But it never got anywhere, I was too chicken to ask her out. Total failure.

I was desperate to get a girlfriend, so my next conquest didn't go much further. By this time, Mr Pearson had retired and a new boss came – Mr Hall. He lived in the park lodge with his ample, buxom wife and his equally buxom daughter. She was fifteen or sixteen, I recall, not very good looking, but most of the time I wasn't looking at the colour of her eyes! Still at school, but I plucked up courage to ask her out. She said, 'Yes,' but I told her not to tell her dad who she was going out with, just to tell him that she was going out with some school friends or something. So we arranged to go to the pictures one night. She turned up at our arranged meeting place, but to my horror she was wearing her school uniform and carrying a satchel. She said she had told her dad that she was going to a friend's house to do some homework. Needless to say, this didn't go down well with me, but what could I do? We went to the pictures – I remember it was the Palladium cinema. I forgot the film, I wasn't that bothered, I just wanted to know what "they" felt like. But I didn't even try. Again I chickened out. My third attempt came a little later. It involved college, but I'll pick that up in my next chapter.

Three years or so had passed since I started work. I was, by this time, coming to like my job more and more. After all the leg-pulling and jokes, I got on famously with my work buddies and was now starting, at last, to learn my trade. I started, as it was, to be taught "in house" by Ray. He held classes every Saturday morning when he was on weekend duty from about 10am until 12.30pm. He would show anyone his skills, around ten lads would turn up voluntarily for tuition in plot work, propagation and mechanics. He was also a gadget man and a bit of an experimenter. Making coffee from dandelion roots and chicory, making his own tobacco from dried Nicotiana leaves which he used to grow laced with mint and herbs. He also multi-grafted chrysanths so that you ended up with different coloured blooms on one root stock. He was a very intelligent man who could turn his hand to anything. Very gentle, soft spoken – everybody had time for Ray.

He died Preston Guild week, 1972, a great loss. His teaching gave me a thirst for more gardening information and I became the 'blue-eyed boy' all of a sudden when I asked if I could go to college on day release. The Council paid my tuition and I began a 4-year horticultural course at Hutton College. Not only did this set me on the road to qualifications, but I opened up, be it only one day a week. It brought me into contact with other students (maybe girls as well). Studying with others from local towns, we had a ball.

Doing both practical and principal work, I loved it, gaining ULCI, GCE and City & Guilds qualifications on the way. But it had little relevance to what I was doing at work. That was sort of stuck in a time warp, but I was happy with the situation. Work at Miller and Avenham parks and greenhouses had a yearly cycle and college filled in all the background. We studied botany, genetics, entomology, pathology and design. I loved it all. Going to college was a real blast, but I took advantage of being a student (be it only day release) lifestyle.

We would attend horticultural college in the morning and then go back into town for a chippy lunch followed by a 1½ hour lesson on botany at Preston's Harris College. We were then allowed 1½ hour liberal studies to help break our long day (which also included night school) at Trinity College which was about a ten minute walk from the Harris College, but it hardly ever happened. Someone had the idea that if we get our skates on, we could be at the Castle Vernon Bowling Alley in fifteen minutes, have a game then back to the Harris – brilliant idea! So ten lads went hell for leather to get the best score. The winner got to wear a white peaked flat cap with large black spots on it and had to wear it for the rest of the day. I wore it with pride on two occasions. I must have looked a bit of an idiot, but I didn't care.

What a trophy.

At about 5pm or so, we would make our way back to the Harris for tea in the canteen. Real good grub and cheap. Time for a break in the college's common room before evening class. It was an occasion when a lot of the students came together from different subjects to chat and get chatted up. One of our group, "Fred", thought he was God's gift and went for a wash and brush up before joining us as he had spied a 'looker' the week before and said he was going to "pull".

Fred arrived, hair slicked and smelling like an eastern knocking shop with a new college scarf slung loosely around his neck, carrying the latest Cat Stevens LP. Sitting with us for ten minutes or so, the girl with a couple of mates came in. A couple of deep breaths, Fred said, 'Look and learn.' He strutted over to her and sat on the opposite chair. He tried his best to get her chatting, but she wasn't interested. Feeling a bit frustrated, he said, 'Look, do you want a date or not?'

'Piss off,' she said.

'Snotty cow,' he replied and came back to us saying. 'Not my type anyway.'

He suffered more embarrassment as we all fell about laughing.

We had a break at about 7.30pm for 1/2 hour. We could have gone to the common room for a brew, but opted instead to run to the Globe pub next door to college – a real student's hangout for a very swift pint. And swift it was, too, getting back at spot on 8pm for the final hour or so.

The final fling of the day after college was to walk into town to a real cool coffee bar called The Black Cat Club. We would all pile in flashing our college scarves and membership cards which would allow us into the "back room". It was always packed with students all trying to act cool saying things like, "Hi man", "What's hanging", "What's crisp". The back room also sported a brilliant juke box where Sandi Shaw, Gerry, The Kinks and the Stones got a good thrashing. One of our group, called McIver, was from Blackpool – a real, long-haired weirdo, he was our God. I wonder what happened to him, probably ended up living in a commune on Mars or something.

After the second year tuition it was time for exams. A lot of swotting and 3 days of exams resulted with my exam papers being scrapped by the college, much to my upset. I was to go to the principles room to find out why. He said that, 'Unfortunately the college didn't receive the exam charges from my employer.' So, not only were my papers cancelled, I had to go through the whole of the second year again. I wasn't happy.

Back at work, I received an apology from the council – an administration error. Still, there was nothing I could do, so I was 'back yeared'. This was certainly a turning point for me. I was in the second year for a second time, meeting students who had all come up from the first year. Amongst the class were 2 girls – Pauline and Olwyn. I got chatting to Pauline one break time and felt really comfortable with her. A smile or 2 from her made me feel on top of the world. I picked up courage to ask her out and she said, 'Yes.' Boy, I skipped home that night. To cut a long story short, very short for now, we dated for about 2 years, got engaged and we married in July 1970. We'd been together for forty-two blissfully happy years and have 2 children. We were extremely content with each other – best friends, soul mates and lovers, until she was cruelly taken away by cancer at the age of sixty-two. A wonderful, beautiful, gentle lady the world and myself lost.

Back to college, well, the second year went a breeze, third and fourth. I was then entered to go to Calderstones Park in Liverpool to take the top exam at that time. The first grade Certificated Gardeners Exam. This I passed with 3 credits and 2 distinctions. The park superintendent, Mr Hall, had left by this time and had gone to Australia and was replaced by Mr Jones – an ex-army type, beer belly as well. He was pleased with my results and suggested I furthered my horticultural education and go for a National Diploma in Horticulture and then probably Landscape Design if I wanted to. So I applied to the regius keeper at Edinburgh Botanic Garden for a 4 year course. Because of the recommendation from Mr Jones and Mr Kay (he was the deputy boss) who had himself achieved NDH from Wisley Horticultural College and my excellent exam results, to my surprise, I was accepted. But my affections were split, not only by this, but also I was looking forward to getting married the following year.

I was very happy working where I was, so I decided not to go on for further education. A decision I wasn't to regret as my life was a pleasure, not only at work, but at home as well. I was a contented lad.

CHAPTER 8
ASHTON BOUND

A vacancy had arisen at our sister nursery at Ashton Park, about a fifteen minute ride away. I applied and got it, basically because only I put in for it. I would be working with Alan Jones, the charge hand – a bachelor still living with his mum, he had a secret lady friend, but everyone knew. It exposed me to a new set of faces on the adjoining park, again a few characters I'll explain later. My job at Ashton was to be Alan's labourer, but I must admit by this time, I think I probably knew more about plant propagation than he did.

Being there gave me a chance to get on to greenhouse duty, whereby I had to go back to nursery every night, seven days a week to make adjustments to the venting system and boilers so that the plants would be okay for the night. Alan ran the nursery to supplement the plants that would be needed for parks bedding schemes and floral decoration work. Every greenhouse was kept spotlessly clean, no plant out of position in fact. When Henry came for plants for decoration work, Alan used to get annoyed because he mucked up the benches. It was an idyllic life there and on the odd occasion would go out in the wagon to help out on décor jobs, this I really took too in a big way. It wasn't long before I was putting my own slant on things. I felt now I was really getting out of being a nipper and doing more horticultural work.

Back on the home and social scene, I was getting the taste for a bit of alcohol, in some cases quite a lot and fancied a change in appearance. My hair always called for careful attention and went from the sublime, short(ish) back and sides, to long, but it refused to, it just went sideways, a bit like Coco the clown, but I was scared of getting it cut. As long as I put plenty of Cossack hair spray on, it behaved itself, although it went as solid as a rock. My drinking buddy was Colin, another park worker, and we had many adventures worthy of another book. He had a crew cut one day, I thought he really looked cool and hard, just the look I wanted, so I decided to have the same. Colin decided he would cut it for me and save a bit of money. My mother went on holiday and left me home alone, so I decided to have a home trim after a Friday night skinful. Arriving home, I sat on a kitchen chair in the middle of the living room floor with a bath towel around my neck. I trusted Colin, but he was no barber and even worse when he couldn't see straight and had difficulty standing up. So, off he went with a pair of kitchen scissors and a comb. The result was terrible, it looked like I had been extremely ill.

'Just keep still and I'll straighten it up,' he said.

If ever you've seen the worst case of alopecia, you haven't – you should have seen me. I had to go to work with my woolly hat on in the middle of summer. I looked a right tit. Mum came home on the following weekend and asked why I was wearing it. I took it off and she had a fit.

'Who the bloody hell cut that?' she said.

I had to come clean. So I took myself off to "Little Ted's", a barber on Plungington Road near my house. When I took my hat off, he said, 'Well, whatever I do it's only going to improve.' He almost scalped me, I looked like a convict.

A guy came to help out at Ashton, because we were getting very busy. His name was Brian and he used to work at a nearby park. Brian and I got on famously and have been friends for over forty years now. Alan didn't think much of Brian; I think that was because he was upsetting his apple cart by bringing new blood into his organised military-style way of working. Alan took advantage of the two lads, in fact, he became a bit lazy as on most summer afternoons he would go and watch the old boys bowling on the adjacent greens while we worked. He played at nights for Ashton A team with the park foreman, Tommy. He was an old farmer-type who liked to hear the sound of his own voice. He and Alan were the best of enemies.

One day, Tommy went off with a bad back. He lived in the park house, but nothing was seen or heard of him when one of the lads went round to ask some instruction. He came back the day after making a remarkable recovery. The day after that, he almost had a coronary when the headline in that evening's newspaper said:

"Tom reaches final in Waterloo"

He had, in fact, gone to Blackpool, practised all day and got through the quarter and semi-finals. It got to the desk of Mr Jones and "they had words".

Another chap who worked at Ashton park was called Mr Hunt. He was a tractor driver. He always dressed like a tramp, lived very, very cheaply, but some say was worth a fortune. He was "Mr One Speed" – if his arse was on fire, he wouldn't run for the nearest bucket of water – he was always slow. Indeed, his tractor hardly ever got out of second gear. He used to wear his clothes until they wore out before replacing them, and I mean "wear out". He always wore a ganzy (a jumper) – the front was so well worn, he used to darn it with any wool he could lay his hands on, until it was thoroughly worn out. One day, we thought he had a new jumper on, but it was the same one back to front. 'Another twelve months left in it,' he'd say. His trousers were held up with a bit of rope and his old trench coat probably came from the trenches. He never hurried to do anything. His motto was 'If you can't do it today, do it tomorrow. If you can't do it tomorrow, f*** it.'

Working at Ashton wasn't easy. Brian and I made many tons of potting compost by hand and everything handled seemed to be heavy. Every Friday, one of us would have to clean the boilers – they were like a ship's engine room – all polished brass and copper, even the boiler coats were painted. The floors were scrubbed and mopped.

Brian left after a couple of years. He went to work on the council's "tree gang". Replacing him was a guy called Bidmead – his nickname was 'Biddy'. Unknown to us at the time, Biddy wasn't a full shilling, if you know what I mean. A can short of a six pack, he unfortunately had mental problems. He didn't last long after trying to stab Alan the foreman with a garden hoe, then smashing loads of glass in the greenhouses. We had to call in the authorities – 2 men in white coats and an ambulance picked him up. The last time I heard he was in a mental hospital, somewhere near Lancaster I think.

It was while I was at Ashton that we got involved with flower shows. During the past few years, being involved in floral decoration jobs, we thought we were pretty good as we had been doing jobs not only for the civic functions, but also the Mayoral ball, registrar's office and different venues around town. But we never competed in flower shows against other towns and organisations. So in the mid-seventies, Mr Jones entered Preston Parks into the Southport Flower Show. We designed a Maltese cross decked out with all manner of flowering plants. Most of the design was done by the lads as the foreman, Harry, didn't want anything to do with it. I think, now, because it was way out of his comfort zone, for he wasn't a chap to embrace new ideas and innovations. Alan, the charge hand, didn't fare much better. He put in his penny's worth of ideas, but they were not very inspiring.

A chance to travel across the border all fourteen miles to Southport seemed very exciting and a chance to see what other towns could do. So we put on our first show – a twenty foot by twenty foot display. We managed to get a silver gilt medal for our efforts and were quite proud of it, also receiving a £50 cheque as well. But I wanted more, seeing other displays by the likes of the Royal parks, Liverpool, Belgium and even Japan and South Africa at one stage gave me a thirst for bigger and better. A chance to adapt and change the way we used plants in more innovative ways using props, lights, water and sound would give the public, and hope the judges too, a feel of what we really could achieve.

The following few years we nicked and changed other people's ideas and used them in our own displays as well as brand new designs by ourselves. Competing on this scale brought vast improvements in design, as in following years we never achieved less than gold medals and a smattering of large gold medals. But just when we were reaching the top of the tree, all flower show designs were stopped. It was on our last display that a member of Preston Council came to visit us at Southport (we had received a large gold on that occasion) and he and Fred Jones had words. The councillor said to Fred, 'A good show, Fred, but it's a pity the parks look a mess.' It was at a time when, not only ourselves, but other boroughs and town parks were on a decline and didn't think it right that Preston was paying for us to go on a "jolly" to the seaside while the parks suffered. So that was the end of that. We didn't compete for another twenty years or so.

Brian and myself then took it upon ourselves to keep new ideas going and once a year we went over the top – really developing new ideas to include in Preston's annual Mayoral Ball. Developing waterfalls, grottos, even reusing old props made for Southport and making new ones. Using water in displays brought sound, movement and a natural charm to our ideas, and it was loved by everyone. Our proudest moment came in 1977 at the celebration of the Queen's Silver Jubilee when we were given the free run to do a decoration in our Guild Hall for the visit by Her Majesty. The whole stage back was decked out as well as the sixty foot frontage, as well as areas in the town hall. It looked stunning and we knew it. Just to change the subject here, it was the same year that Brian had a vasectomy, a brave thing to do. His wife had gone through a tough time, so they decided it was a good thing to do after having two boys. This got me thinking about why I think I'll have it done as by then Pauline and I had 2 children. We didn't want any more, so why not? I'll let my next rhyme tell the story.

A VASECTOMY TALE

Several years ago you know,
I decided to have it done,
Because I didn't want any more kids
Apart from my daughter and son.

The day before the operation,
I had to shave my stem
And what a sorry sight it looked
Hanging like a fresh plucked hen.

The day arrived, so did the nerves
And with a "Good luck" from the wife
Off I went to hospital
To meet the surgeon's knife.

It didn't take long, just twenty mins
Then someone else's turn
To have a scalpel shoved in the groin
To separate them from sperm.

I felt dead proud when it was done
As I had completed one of my goals.
No ill effects and life carried on,
Apart from slightly achy balls.

The problem was 3 months later,
For I had to produce a sample,
But sperm on demand, from the wife's warm hand
Produced nowt, I didn't feel ample.

For it wouldn't rise no matter what.
I used methods of every type.
It just hung limp and lifeless,
Like an empty wobbly pipe.

So with literally a tale between my legs,
I set off early to work
And telling my mate what I couldn't do
Make me feel a nerk.

He said, 'I will help you, you're my mate.'
He said he'd do what I can't.
I looked at him with fear and dread
And said, 'No, you bloody won't.'

He then spelled out a fool proof plan
As he really meant to help me.
So get tut bog with your sample bottle
And take a look at today's page 3.

So there I was, perched on't bog
Feeling a little silly
Looking at Julie stuck on the door
And playing with my willy.

Well after much ado, I had an eruption.
It was success indeed.
So thanks to Julie from page 3,
I had my bottle of seed.

We set off, hot foot straight away
Driving as fast as we can
To take my stuff to the hospital lab
In our parks department van.

All proved well with the tadpole test.
That really gave me a break.
So that's the story of what happened to me
And my one-eyed trouser snake.

Yes indeed, the best fifty quid I ever spent.

CHAPTER 9
BACK AT MILLER

A couple of years later, I found myself back at Miller after Harry retired and Alan had then become foreman. The sky high position as charge hand was then handed to me. In my charge at Miller was Brian and Joan. She was a redeployed worker from a local, private plant nursery that shut down. There was also an old guy called Ernie. Ernie seemed a bit of an oddball. He was so old-fashioned in his ways, everything he did was methodical every day – sweeping the path from the bosses house whether it needed it or not, feeding the 2 cats Snowy and Tiddles. Tiddles, a black cat, was scared of its own shadow and would run a mile from anyone exception Ernie. Snowy was so damn fat from too much Whiskas that if a mouse run over its head it wouldn't bat an eyelid. As a treat for the cats, each Friday when Brian and myself went out to maintain our permanent decorations in civic buildings, Ernie asked us to get some fish for the cats. His order was always the same – £1 of coley fish (I think it's also called rock salmon) from Tom and Alice's fish stall on our local market. So he would boil up this fish in an old pan until the flesh fell off the bones. The cats used to do somersaults and the place stank of fish. They would gobble up as much as they could until they couldn't move. But before going home at night, he would clean the dishes of old fish and fill 'em up again with Whiskas. Many Monday mornings that was still in the dishes. Anyway, both cats snuffed it after a year or two, but we didn't get any more, thank God!

Fishing used to be (and still is) a great pastime of Brian and I, so we had this brilliant idea of producing our own maggots. At least we would save about £2 a week. So on our next outing to the fish stall, we asked Tom and Alice if they could let us have a couple of cod heads, they were only going to get thrown anyway. Back at base, these would be kept in a shady place so that flies could lay their eggs on them – it didn't take long, just a few hours. The fish heads were then wrapped in newspaper and placed in the dark in the bottom of an old dustbin. These were then left for at least a week when the eggs hatched and began to feed on the heads. By this time, things started to get a bit ripe, but we continued to feed the young maggots by giving them a couple more fish heads the week after. Just for a change, we would throw in the odd tin of Whiskas as well.

By two weeks, it really hummed so strong of ammonia it made you wretch. Then came the time to sieve them from the dustbin – a difficult job because they were wet and stuck and crawled all over the place. They had to be handled one by one as they wouldn't just pour out of the bin. There were thousands of them. We were clearly doing something wrong, all the time the smell would make our hair stand on end. While we were dealing with the operation, Fred the boss came down the path from the house, so we had to pretend to be doing something else and trying to divert him from the bins. He was about twenty-five yards away when we caught him before he got any further.

'There seems to be a queer smell coming from somewhere,' he said.

Well, trying to look puzzled, 'Must be a dead rat or something,' I said. 'I'll try and find it and bury it.'

'Good show,' and off he went.

Well, this called for an executive decision by us and we decided to suspend operations at Miller, it was too dangerous, so we moved our fledgling industry to Ashton boiler house. This we did the next week, but things went from bad to worse. On organising the boiler room and depositing a load of fish heads in a bin, we went away feeling pretty confident this time. Not only were we trebling our output, we were doing it in secret as well. The trouble came the next week going to see how our industry was progressing. On opening the boiler house door, we saw literally thousands of maggots crawling all over the place. It absolutely stank and with no way of collecting them, we had to close down operations. We failed big style, all for the sake of saving £2 a week.

It wasn't the first time we tried to make a quick quid. Another time saw us trying to corner the market in logs for burning. The tree gang used to dump all their trees and stuff under the bridge at Avenham. Sometimes there were great heaps of the stuff – tons of it. So, it occurred to us that if we could get permission to use them for our own use, we would be quids in if we could sell it. Brian had a small chainsaw and we would cut wood each weekend, bag it and sell it to whoever wanted any for £1 a bag. Finding customers was a matter of asking anyone we came into contact with. Filling twenty bags took some doing, chain sawing the logs into splittable pieces was hard work. So, after a few hours graft, plus petrol for the car and delivering we made about £10 each, so this enterprise didn't make us much money either. We seem to have had illusions of grandeur, thinking we could corner the market in logs.

Our self-styled motto was STEL EB NIOD or looked at another way (backwards) it read LETS BE DOIN. Well, that soon hit the skids as well. Ever the entrepreneurs, another project seemed a goer as we had then entered compulsive contract tendering (CCT) stage and had to compete for our own work by the orders of the government. Unfortunately, the council parks bedding plant production was lost out to Leeds City Council, but they couldn't deliver the required amount of plants at the required specification. So, we had to go shopping locally for 30,000 plants. We succeeded with a bit of effort. This left our own greenhouses empty and we were just waiting for someone to fill them. Brian and I got permission from our boss to grow our own as long as we used our own time and materials. And so we did with a few visits to wholesale suppliers, spending a few hundred pounds and working a few evenings and weekends. We soon found willing customers and delivering in late spring brought rewards. After paying tax on our profits as market traders, Brian bought some double glazing and I bought a nice fire surround – solid wood as well. Pleased with our third-time-lucky success, we called ourselves "Lazy Acres" and had sweat shirts made with our logo on. This continued for 2 more years, but it was getting too big for us, and besides, the council started growing our own again, so we decided to let it go. It was good while it lasted, though.

There was a time when Brian and I almost became famous in our own boiler house. One winter's afternoon we both decided that the boilers could do with a good cleaning. It was always a dirty job scrubbing out the flues with a long brush. Getting rid of all the fall from the chimney was a nightmare with choking dust everywhere. Anyway, at least it was warm. The boiler room was underneath the mess room in a dark, dreary cellar with hardly any ventilation. The electric fan had packed up ten years ago. The cellar was lit with sixty watt bulb on a clip plugged into the kettle socket upstairs. Brian used to bring in his cassette recorder and we would listen to tapes whilst we cleaned. One favourite tape was *The Best of Manfred Mann*. We played it over and over again, belting out the words we knew off by heart. We made a particularly good job of the boilers that day, so we began to spruce the cellar up as well. I found an old tin of red paint and a tin of white, but not enough of each to paint the walls one colour. So, mixing them together, we managed a large tin of sickly pink. This was slapped on the walls and finished off with a spider's web painted in a bit of black paint that was hanging around. It began to look good, but tacky. All the while, Manfred Mann was playing, so we created a couple of microphones out of old photo-electric cells and a bit of old wiring taped onto brush handles. To complete the scene, a spade and a shovel became guitars. Setting the wired bulb with an aluminium pie dish behind it became the spot light.

The stage was 2 old pallets, and so "The Idiots" took to the stage doing some fancy moves, miming to "Do Wha Diddy Diddy". After ten minutes sound-check and practise, we were ready for our first gig. So our invited audience of Joan and Ernie and a cat came to watch. For a load of rubbish, we weren't bad. If only Brian Epstein had been there that day, we might have been able to tour the world. Well, it worked for another group. Now, what was their name?

I have often heard of parts of the adjacent park being frequented by ghosts and strange happenings. Such as at dawn on some mornings cow bells could be heard quite clearly making their way along the river bank which runs along the park boundary. Other sightings have also been reported of a seemingly lost dog running across the lawns and then disappearing. I have also heard the story of a couple of ghosts sitting on a seat that isn't there, just staring across the park. But one such happening I can really relate to happened one October morning in the early nineties. At the time, I was working by myself in the greenhouses and so, to get a bit of company for a while, I would make my way into the park to join the lads for brew time. If I hadn't have done that, I probably wouldn't have seen or spoken to anyone all day. Anyway, it was a particularly bad morning weather wise – heavy rain and quite dull. On nearing the mess room, I heard a commotion coming from the brew shed about ten yards away as I was approaching. A little dog, a mongrel named Jack who lived in the park house with the supervisor, came screaming down from there as though he had been kicked and scolded. He passed me at a rate of knots, tail between his legs, still making a screaming noise. I really thought someone had hit him, poor thing. He disappeared down into the park and was not seen again for the rest of the day. I approached the mess room to find all the lads in one of the sheds looking around with puzzled looks.

'Who kicked the dog?' I asked.

'Did you see that?' Steve said.

'See what?' All I saw was Jack hot-footing into the park.

While the lads were under the shed, all of them said they clearly saw a man dressed in a floor length, black coat and a floppy hat gliding up the path towards them into the mess room. We all gingerly walked the few yards and peeped in. All we saw was one of the other lads painting some small fence panels that were to be used for the British Legion garden in a couple of weeks' time.

He looked at us and said, 'What's up with you?'

'Where is he?'

'Who?'

'The tall guy in black.'

'Don't know what you're talking about.'

So, seemingly the spook had walked right past the lads and entered the mess room where he had just disappeared. Something told me these guys didn't make it up as their faces told the story. And I certainly don't think Jack made it up, either.

In later years, other strange things happened in that old mess room where I used to have my break at the greenhouses. Having lunch one day, the sliding door simply slid back all by itself. There was no one about and the weather was good, so no drought would have done it. Of course, it's my word against everybody else's, but it is quite true. The same place has also been witness to our radio crackling quite bad followed by a real icy blast and a whistle. The last occasion, it was not long after the last one, I was whistling while working in there and a clear noise like someone said, 'Sshhh.' Both Brian and I really did feel a presence on those occasions, but nothing since.

This next tale must have seen me as the luckiest guy in Preston that day. A friend of Brian's used to own a photography business doing all kinds of work – weddings, photos for estate agents, all sorts. One day, he came to the greenhouse to ask if he could do some photography to test out some new lenses under normal light conditions using colour wheels and a whole list of other things. We mentioned it to the boss at the time. He seemed very uninterested and said, 'OK.' So Tony, the photographer, arrived a few days later in his estate car and proceeded to get out all the gear. We helped him get up a 'bit of a set' in the tropical house – blue backcloth, arranging a good selection of palms and stuff. Just as we were finishing that, he set up his cameras and a couple of lights when I heard another car approaching. Out of it stepped what I would describe as 2 of the most beautiful girls.

Tony said, 'I got the help of two girls as well to help me with skin tones as well. I hope you don't mind.'

'Mind! Ah, well, no.'

'Can the girls change somewhere?'

'Well, we only had the toilet area at the end of the office, it will have to do.'

So they went to get changed, or must I say, undressed.

They appeared ten minutes later with just dressing gowns on and then proceeded to touch up their make-up. With a final adjustment to cameras, Tony said, 'OK girls.'

They took off their gowns and all they were wearing was biking bottoms, nothing else. Posing amongst the foliage and back drop, they were holding a multi-coloured beach ball and a beach brolly, amongst other things. Well, I tried my best to look uninterested, but the beast in me thought otherwise. I couldn't keep my eyes off them. Well, I'm only human!

Brian, by this time, had noticed what was going on from outside the greenhouses. If he had come in, it would have been obvious he just wanted a good gander. So he went to the end of the greenhouse and rubbed 2 little spy holes into the greenhouse shading, 'Just to see if everything was going to plan, of course.'

After about an hour of adjustments and clicking the camera, Tony asked if I could do him a favour. Could I please turn the hosepipe on and create a mist to cover the girls as this would, of course, wet their hair and create a different skin tone. Well, in the immortal words of 007 in *Octopussy*, I thought, 'I must be dreaming.' This I did without being asked twice. A few more shots later and it was job done. After towelling themselves dry and putting dressing gowns back on, we just sat and chatted while Tony packed up his things. The two girls were from a local model agency and very pleasant. We shared a joke or two. A few days later, Tony appeared again asking to use the greenhouse again.

'No problem.'

When he appeared, he did so with a van with nothing more than a few bits of conservatory furniture. All done within a couple of hours and left. He never did return, but left us with a memory fit for this book and all done in 'the best possible taste'. That particular week ended with me going fishing on the Saturday afternoon. It was a glorious day, but unfortunately I didn't catch anything. But on that day, it was one that really stuck in my mind for some reason. I was sitting in the car at the end of the day, thinking what a wonderful job I was in. Working with lovely people, working with the seasons, each season bringing its own joys, sometimes frustrations, but all the while being so absorbing. My life, to then, being pure joy. There wasn't much money, but so rich in health, a wonderful family – indeed, there was nowhere on earth that I would rather have been at that particular time. So much so, that I composed this short poem. It was scribbled down on my rod licence envelope. I still have it!

PEACE

Finding peace for myself is so easy
For it's here by the water's edge
Amongst the trees and wildlife
The balsam, the reeds, the sedge.
There's movement, song and silence.
On the breeze, there is sweet scented air
From the flowers of waterside willows.
There for me and nature to share.
This gives me everything that I want.
I'll take nothing from its treasure,
Except memories of gentle things
And a peaceful mind of pleasure.

From time to time, the council invites our twin town equals from Germany, France or Poland. On one occasion, they invited, as part of an exchange, delegates from our German twin town of Recklinghausen. We did all the usual tidying up bit, but unfortunately, the night before the planned visit, our Miller Park's ornate flower urns were smashed by vandals. Some of these had been smashed before and repaired, but a couple were original pieces dating back to 1865. The park lads tidied up as best they could, but the vandalism was there for all to see. I was chosen as part of a welcoming committee to be in the park on their arrival, as well as the mayor and a couple of our management. Sure enough, at 11am, a few cars made their way into the park. The dignitaries got out and began to wander about, the park's management pointing out, via a translator, all of the many features and history. They came to where I was then said the usual welcome, shook hands, smiled and then started to explain what had gone on. What I said next rates amongst the top ranks of mastery of the unfortunate phrase, saying I was sorry to find us in a bit of a mess as last night we were blitzed. A stony silence, a forced semi-smile from the German representative made me instantly think, 'Oh shit, what have I said?' It felt like Basil from *Fawlty Towers* "Don't mention the war". I nearly did.

Quickly moving on, the delegates made their way to lunch. What I said didn't spark an international incident, but was the cause of much amusement and piss taking from the other guys present. I don't recall the German's ever coming back while I was there. I don't know why?

Fred Jones, the superintendent, was known to be a bit of a drinking man, mainly Bells whiskey, but he also did a bit of home brewing of wine for himself and his wife, Freda. On occasions, Fred took a little more beverage at the wrong time. You could always tell – he was over joyful, laughing at nothing and staggering about was a bit of a giveaway. Prior to the grass cutting season, we used to employ a few extra workers to help with seasonal tasks. This occasion saw Fred, along with the head of personnel, interviewing in the office. Now Fred had been on the tipple for most of the morning when the head of personnel arrived. Setting up the office, it was suggested a good idea if Fred would move his 4 large demijohns (which were all bubbling away merrily on a makeshift shelf above his radiators) before interviews began. This was done by myself and taken to the warm greenhouse where they continued to bubble away merrily. Fred was well-oiled when the first candidate turned up and the interviews began. Apparently, he wasn't making much sense and fell off his chair. Personnel had to apologise to the interviewee and made up an excuse that Fred was unwell. It was decided to cancel him out of the interviews for the rest of the day.

It wasn't long after that that Fred retired and everything started to change. All the old ways had to go as we entered a new dawn of fresh management. A very young boss with a posse of likewise undermanagers changed the system from top to bottom. One assistant, straight from college – clean nails, suit and tie – I could never take to him, a right smart arse. Looked like he never broke out in a sweat his entire life, said he was going to bring the park back to its original splendour.

'Well,' I said, 'there's a barrow and spade, get on with it.'

It wasn't long before he found pastures new.

One story that always amuses me was about the same time when things had to be politically correct and we seemed to be losing the banter and a sense of fun. New offices were created and desks in the new leisure department were blocked off with partitions. Instead of just turning around to ask a colleague something, they had to use internal phones to speak to someone 2 yards away. A bit like *The Apprentice* on TV where Sir Alan Sugar phones the secretary 3 yards away to send in the candidates. Anyway, a lot of internal mail was flying about. One day, I was asked to deliver a large envelope to the administration desk from our park office. I arrived at the offices with the envelope which had 'Admin' on it. I couldn't resist a joke. On arriving at reception, I asked if they had an Asian guy working here by the name of Admin.

'There's no one by that name here,' came the reply.

'Well, I have an envelope for Admin, can you please check?'

I thought the penny might have dropped, but no, off she went looking for him. Nobody twigged, so I had to come clean.

'I think its short for administration,' I said.

Nobody saw the funny side. Why not? Is it me that has a strange sense of humour, or do they not have any?

I never really took to the new order of things, least of all the new manager. He was brought in to be a real hatchet man. He was mostly disliked by the lads. When he left a few short years later, after causing mayhem, the usual good luck card went the rounds for signing. It came to my comment and I wrote "Bloody good riddance". When the director in charge read my comment, as he was the last to sign it, he called for me to see him. On entering his office, he said, holding up the card, 'Did you write this?'

'Yes,' I replied.

'Well, you're the only one who told the bloody truth. Shut the door on your way out.'

All the rest had put the usual "Miss you", "Good luck" and all that crap. I felt rather pleased with myself. A new era had definitely arrived. We didn't have a boss as in a name now, but in "deputy director", John. His office desk was likened to a fitted kitchen – everything in its place, extremely tidy, as was his car. Over the years, he had several. They always looked clean and shiny – he must have kept Zipwax in business. Slight alterations took place in the office. One that I vividly recall is that one day someone used the loo and left, shall we say, a bit of a hum. This must have been a bit of an embarrassment for John as there was always a rep or two who wanted to use the loo and it didn't create a good impression of the place when it stank like a manure heap. So he thought it good idea to have a wall fan installed. This used to come on when the light was put on. I couldn't resist a rhyme, hope it's not too crude!

ODE TO THE LOO!

If, like me, your poo poo poo's
When you come here for a dump
And things are horribly smelly
That fall out from your rump

Then just make sure the light is on
As this operates the fan
To remove the offending odour
As quickly as it can.

But, I don't know what the fuss is about
When I come here to do my pile
Because I can stand it, although you can't
And I don't think it's vile.

But I will think of others
Who follow me to this bog.
So, I'll turn on the light
Then flush my shite.
No smell and no brown log.

After I wrote this, I pinned it up on the back of the toilet door. It met with much amusement, but had to be taken down prior to any visitors.

A different structure took place. A big shuffle of management. I was asked if I would like to become a supervisor along with another guy. I was to have a car, a radio and a raise in pay. I sounded good, so I took it – a bad mistake. I was really out of my comfort zone dealing with the client side which consisted of new managers, tech assistants, the odd councillor and the public. This was as well as looking after not only the nursery, but 2 parks and mobile gangs. I lasted for about 3 months. By then, I'd had enough and was longing to return to what I did best – growing and showing plants. So, one morning, I returned the keys and radio back to the deputy director. He tried to talk me out of it, but I was determined. The other supervisor also tried to talk me round, but it just wasn't me. I felt a huge weight had been lifted and I don't regret the move back.

The ground maintenance staff, as they were now called, produced some splendid characters – natural comedians, always good lads and real salt of the earth. I used to like talking to them to see what gems of comedy I could ease out of them. But this would come on occasions without being encouraged. People watching is one of the most fascinating things. Most mornings, I would walk down to the garage yard where my van would be parked. All the lads would gather first thing in the morning with everyone taking the rip out of one another. The phone would ring – it would be a supervisor wanting to speak to a particular guy. His name was shouted at full volume from whoever answered the phone, although he was sitting next to the phone. This was to kid the supervisor that whoever it was, was out in the yard preparing for work. Give it ten seconds of quiet, and then answer the phone. It started to click with the supervisor that they were taking the "Mick", so he would enter the yard in his car at 7.30am resulting in a quick scramble. One of the guys, I really thought was such a droll comedian, could have done a turn on stage. On one occasion, I asked if he knew the right time as my watch had stopped. He replied, 'No, I don't. Mine's ten minutes slow!' then walked away. I had to think about that one myself.

One impromptu character I encountered once latched onto me. I was driving the van coming back alone from picking up a few plants and for a short cut was passing a road where, let's say, "ladies of the night" frequented. I was driving slowly between 2 parked cars when my passenger door opened and in jumped a prostitute. "Are you looking for business?"

'No, get out.'

'I'll do you a cheap rate. What time do you finish?'

'Get out.'

She then hitched up her skirt. Well, I have seen thicker pipe cleaners with knots in – she was gross.

'F*** off,' I said.

'And you,' she replied and slammed the door.

On returning to base, I had to tell the lads. To much amusement, one said, 'Oh, that must have been Miss Crabs.'

It happened to us sometimes in that area. Priceless.

CHAPTER 10
TATTON PARK AND RETIREMENT

Although we were kept busy growing plants as required for council use, my favourite jobs by far was designing and constructing floral displays for various functions. The most fun and challenging of these used to be the Southport show displays we did in the 70s. So when a chance of restarting show work came along in 2005, I grabbed it and started to work on it immediately. It was an opportunity to display at Tatton Park Flower Show – a prestigious RHS event in Cheshire that took place every July. The first attempt involved mainly myself and an apprentice. Well, I might as well have done it all myself as he was so hard to motivate. He couldn't care less and didn't understand my enthusiasm. I decided to resurrect a prop that had been in store for about 20 years – a bridge made from larch poles that had been made for Southport flower show years ago. With it, a floral blue stream under it and banks of flowers. On the bridge was boxes filled with purple petunias. I called the display "Bridge over peaceful water".

I found it really hard work and thought people would be keen to give me a lift. It was almost a one man band apart from a couple of lads that helped to pot up the plants a few weeks prior to the show. The same lads helped to construct it and man the stand during the show. After a critical response from the judges, we received a silver medal. I thought then, 'I am not doing this again.' I was frustrated by the lack of interest from certain people. But, enter the following year we did.

By this time, a few more lads jumped on board, but unfortunately we only received a bronze medal for our efforts of "Echoes of Victoriana" and looking at it critically, it was only what we deserved.

There was an increase in enthusiasm in 2005 as Tony joined me in the nursery to construct a display which we called "Preston's French Connection" – a celebration of 50 years between us and our French twin town of Nimes. This resulted in our first gold medal.

Tony really became keen on our flower show designs and set about making a model of our next one which was to be "The Cuerdale Hoard" – an interesting display using a brilliantly constructed Viking boat figure head courtesy of a very talented council joiner, Graham. We made a mock-up of the Viking silver hoard that was originally found on the banks of the River Ribble in Preston during the 1800s. Again a gold medal, plus best exhibit with a prize of a decanter which was proudly received by us all. Our enthusiasm, by this time, saw no boundaries as we were competing with some major players and we were holding our own amongst some of the best in the country. Immediately, we started on 2007's design, which we received permission for by writing to Nick Park, the creator of Wallace and Gromit, and designed a flower bed featuring his characters. Wallace was in bed dreaming of his favourite food – cheese – and Gromit, his faithful pooch, was sat in a rocket setting off to the moon to bring some. This was a very challenging design which Tony again mainly designed, in fact the rocket construction was designed while he was on holiday in Australia. I carved the character heads out of sheets of polystyrene. So keen, I was paper macheing the heads on New Year's Eve. The wife had a glass of wine and I had a bucket of wallpaper paste.

We invited Nick Park to the show and he accepted giving us great reviews. It made TV, radio and the local papers. Nick stayed for quite a while signing autographs and drawing a cartoon on all the photo postcards we had printed. We gave out 3000 cards that week and the display once again won us yet another gold medal.

One of the construction team, Brian, joined us on a permanent basis for the 2008 display as Tony mainly designed our next one which celebrated fifty years since the opening of Britain's first motorway built as the Preston bypass now called the M6. Both Brian and I were not too keen on the idea because it sounded a bit boring. But Tony persisted and designed a wonderful and most imaginative display that again won us gold. That same year saw us doing a show for Southport Flower Show in which we constructed and exhibit featuring one of Ken Dodd's diddymen. We called it "Happiness". This also won us top spot with a cheque of £1000 which disappeared into the council's pot.

The effort we put into these shows was unbelievable. Working at home in the evenings and at weekends it became not just a job, but a complete labour of love. At work, we would argue each other's ideas down, but always came up with a final decision that would have always see us compete with anyone. Unfortunately, the next 5 years were flower show free as it was costing quite a lot to exhibit. It would not have gone down too well in some quarters as job cuts were ‚implemented at that time. We really thought that would be the end of the road as far as the big shows were involved, but we never stopped talking about them. We even came up with a design for Chelsea Flower show and it doesn't get any bigger than that. It would have been a mega challenge and a wonderful thing to be involved with, but it was not to be. We really did miss entering the shows and I still firmly believe that competing is the only way to raise standards.

Continuing to be keen, we visited Tatton on a few occasions just to see what competition there would have been and we were always critical. Although there were some excellent displays, we would not have disgraced ourselves and given them a good run for their money. We were jealous, frustrated and biting at the bit to go back again. So, at the end of 2013, we really bent the management's ear to let us enter again helped by the fact the RHS would give a grant to help us. So, along with this, we said we would come in during our own time to develop the display and they agreed. We put in many hours of thought and work to develop our first show exhibit in 5 years. The diddyman was reborn, but this time we had him at the side of an overflowing treacle well made of plant material. Ken Dodd himself was invited to visit us on site on press day, which he did. A most memorable day that also resulted in us, once again, winning a gold medal. Unfortunately, the number of entries was somewhat down, because all councils were beginning to feel the financial pinch. But we were champing on the bit to do more, our enthusiasm saw no bounds. But again, redundancies were on the cards for many and money was even tighter. I really don't think the 2015 display would have happened if we hadn't once again been a persistent pain in the arse of the management to let us go, promising once again to work in our own time. So, it was permitted, along with a larger grant from the RHS.

Our final fling was to do a display that interpreted the "Battle of Rorks Drift". We called it "Zulu" and it was inspired by the Rev George Smith who was present at the battle and died in Preston. This again, winning us a gold medal and best in show. We sent an invitation to Sir Michael Caine to grace us with his presence at the show, remembering that he played Lt Bromhead in the 1960s film *Zulu*. It would have been something special to have had him on site with us, unfortunately, we wouldn't have been able to pay him anything, but I would have bought him an ice cream – he never replied. He probably doesn't like ice cream!

The last day of the show was my final working day. Although I had officially retired on the 7th July, I kept going in to help out voluntarily to see the show through. I had been preparing myself for retirement for the last few years. Being able to go part time, or tapered retirement as it's called. This really did ease me into retirement as I don't think just finishing work suddenly after 52 years would have done me any favours.

I really did love my job with a passion. It truly became a way of life more than a job to me and reading this book, you might think it was more fooling about and going on jollies. I can assure you, it wasn't. Designing, constructing and displaying plants and flowers, growing millions of plants through the years, keeping all the greenhouses repaired and in order was hard work, but extremely pleasurable. It also gave me the opportunity to work alongside some the best mates anybody could have wished for and most of all being part of the cycle of life. Now that I am approaching my "Saga years", someone told me that meant 'sex annually, generally August' I am looking back with fondest memories and I'm so thankful.

Now that I am fully retired, I must admit that I do miss it, but have no regrets. Being such a manual job has had its merits. I believe it has kept me fit and have a true appreciation of the natural world. We need it, it doesn't need us, all we do is use, abuse it and rearrange it for our own amusement. Having a job working with plants and flowers, I really do have a preference for natural beauty rather than man-made luxury. If day one of my employment with Preston Council was to be tomorrow, I would, without a single doubt, do it all over again.